Victorian North Norfolk Sailing Ships

Michael Stammers

Milepost Research
2012

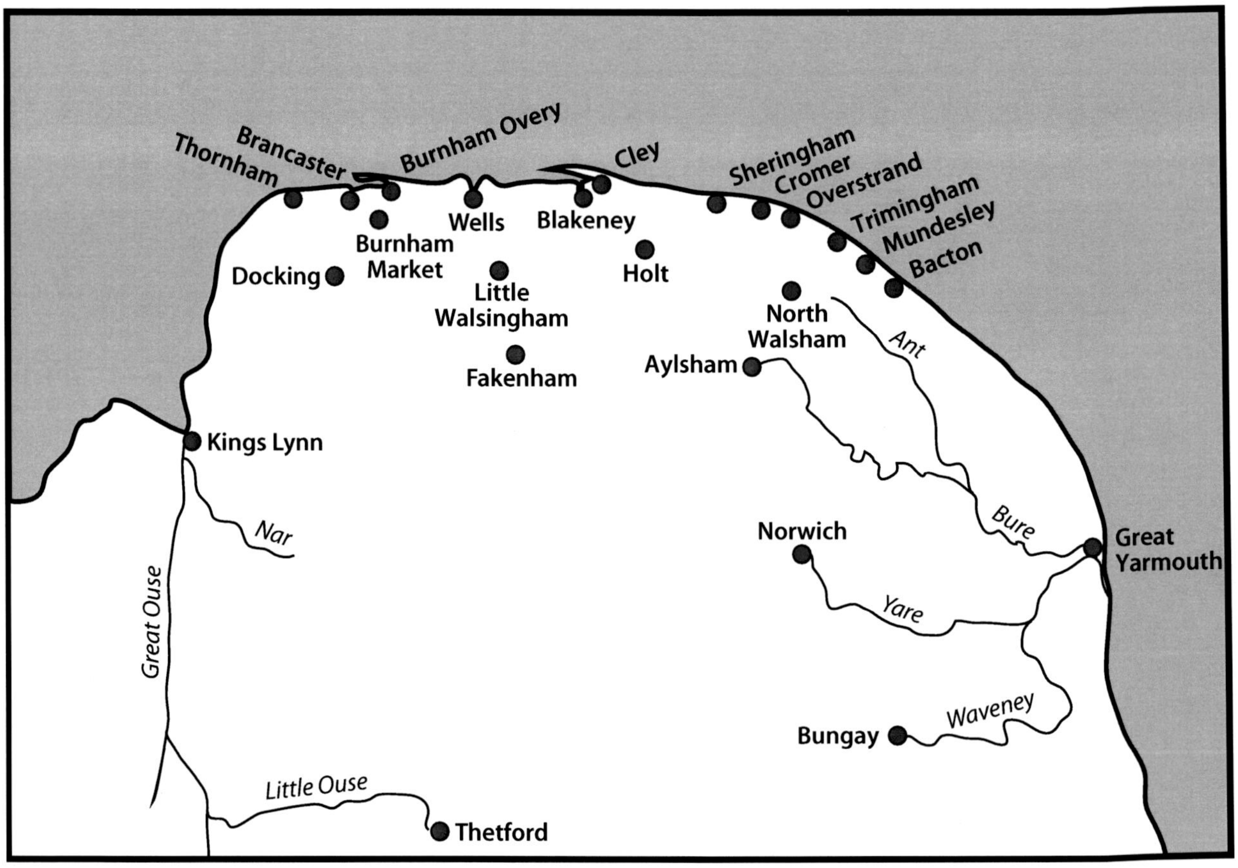

North Norfolk ports and their hinterland in the 19th Century

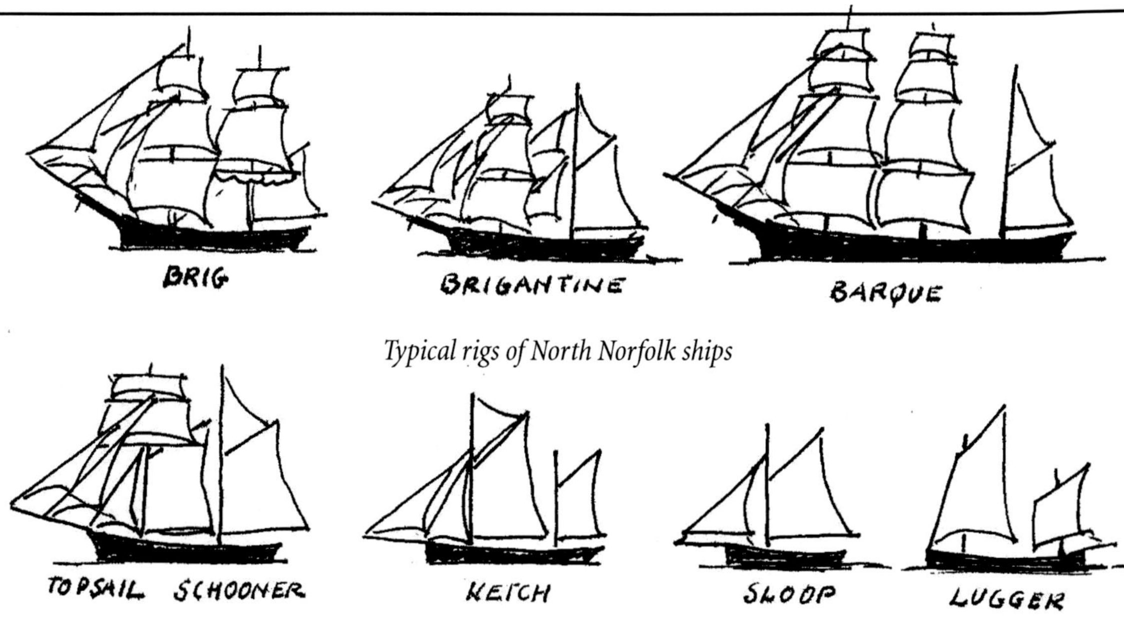

Typical rigs of North Norfolk ships

Victorian North Norfolk Sailing Ships
Published by Milepost Research
tel. 01282 850430; email: mike.clarke@zen.co.uk

ISBN 978 0 9519236-4-4
British Library Cataloguing in Publication Data.
A catalogue record for this book is available from the British Library.

Introduction

This is a record of the ships that were owned in North Norfolk during Queen Victoria's reign. I hope I have made it as complete as possible but the sources make this difficult. I define North Norfolk as running from the haven at Thornham through the beach landing places at Walcott. King's Lynn and Great Yarmouth are excluded and the principal places are Wells, Blakeney and Cley.

The main sources are the Shipping Registers maintained by the Custom Houses. This gave the identifying features of the vessel and who owned it. Every ship's capital could divided in 64 shares. This fraction was a traditional division. There was usually a managing owner who held more shares than his or her fellow investors. As will be seen later on shareholders were a very diverse group but essentially all drawn from the coastal strip. The certificate of registry was the title deed to the ship. The Registers for Wells survive from 1832 and those of Cley from1839. Cley and Wells combined from 1853 to 1855. After that date, the Wells Customs House took responsibility for ship registrations until 1881. The annual numbers had been on the decline and registrations after 1881 were carried out by the King's Lynn Custom House. When I first used these Registers for a school essay, back in 1962, they were housed on the top floor the picturesque Queen Anne Custom House at Lynn. They have since been deposited at the Norfolk Record Office under the file NRO P/SH/L/. One of the quirks of these hand-written volumes is their spellings. Cley is rendered as 'Clay' and Blakeney as 'Blackney'. This suggests that these places were pronounced differently in an early 19th Century Norfolk dialect.

Lloyd's registers and other commercially published registers of shipping do not have the legal standing of the official registers. They were compilations to assist those in shipping or insurance in assessing the condition of a vessel. In the early 19th century they are also far from comprehensive and are especially patchy for coasting vessels. Clayton's

Many North Norfolk vessels were wrecked but others were condemned as unseaworthy and broken up or in the case of the ***GREEK SLAVE*** *abandoned. She was left to rot on the banks of Breydon Water just inland from Great Yarmouth in 1888.*

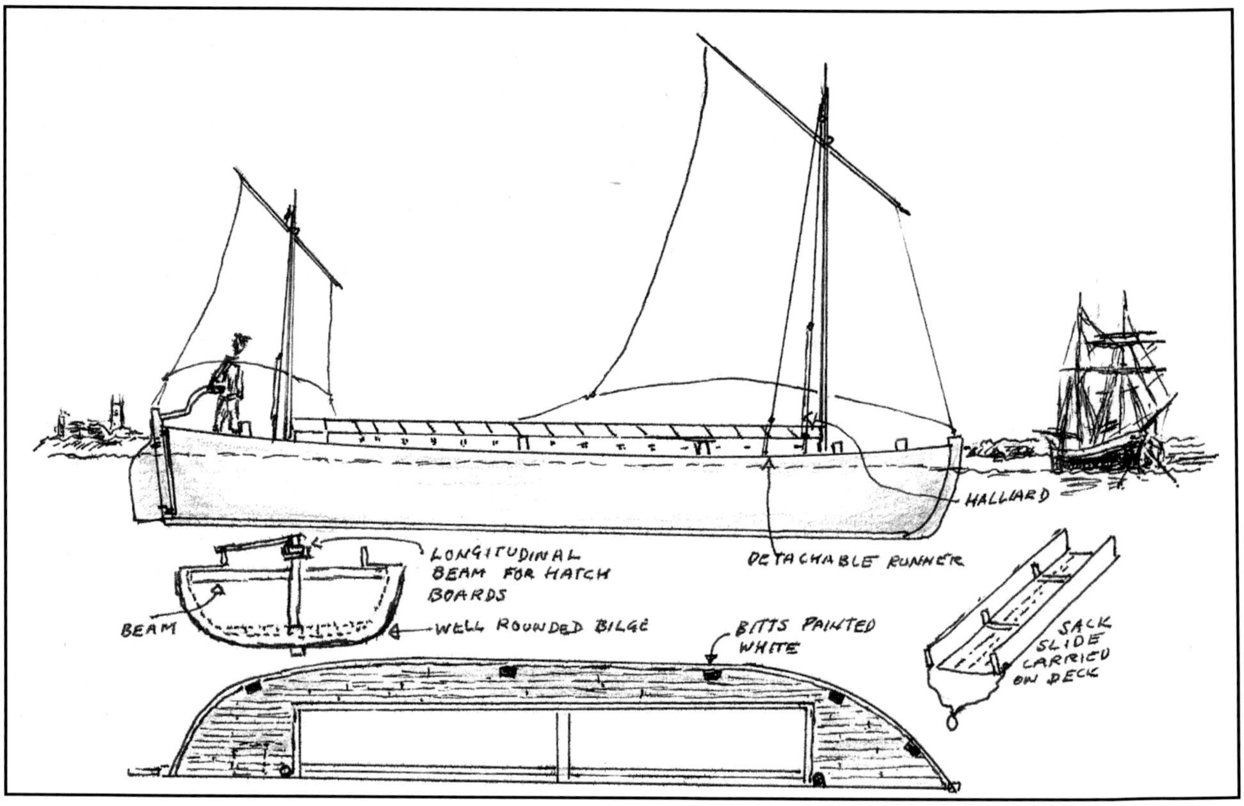

*Plan of the lug-rigged lighter **GLAVEN** built at Blakeney in 1841 for William and Robin Cooke for carrying cargo to and from the Pit anchorage in Blakeney Harbour. There were other lighters in use there but the **GLAVEN** was the only one to be registered.*

Register of 1865 is the most useful as it provides what appears to be a comprehensive list of ships owned in Norfolk ports. But it only appeared once in 1865. Local newspapers such as the ***Norfolk Chronicle*** or the ***Norwich Mercury*** provided 'Marine Intelligence' on the arrivals and sailings at local ports, and these can be supplemented by ***Lloyd's List*** and the Customs Bills of Entry. The latter was published daily at major ports. Both tend to report less on the coasting trade which was the North Norfolk ports' role and more on deep-sea trade. Annual statistics gathered by the Board of Trade also show the extent of locally owned shipping and traffic.

The detail of the master and owners can be enhanced by references in local trade directories and census returns from1841 onwards. It is possible to glean evidence of some of the local business networks that supported local vessels.

They also reveal multiple occupations — a common feature in 19th century commerce, and the real occupations behind the term 'shipowner'. Shipowner in the registers carried with it a certain amount of prestige. Other terms are now unfamiliar; for example, 'clerk' did not mean what it does today, but was a 'clerk in Holy Orders' i.e. a clergyman. Likewise a bricklayer might be a building contractor, or gardener meant marker gardener.

The format of the list roughly follows that of the ship registers but certain features are assumed. Unless mentioned all vessels are carvel built with square sterns. Clench or clinker built hulls were confined to fishing luggers and billy-boys. Also, the number of masts or decks are omitted.The number of masts can be assumed from the rig and the majority were single decked ships. Figureheads and stern decorations are mentioned, but most ships had neither. Tonnages change with changes in measurement rules and tons are rounded up or down as required. Most length, breadth and depth of hold dimensions are given in tenths of feet. Incidentally the third figure, the depth of hold is that and not the draft of the vessel. There was no figurehead unless mentioned.

A small tonnage might imply a fishing smack but it seems even small vessels under 20 tons might be used for cargo, eg. ***Endeavour of Brancaster*** of 1857. Many owners resorted to mortgages to finance their purchase or fund deficiencies elsewhere. Lenders varied and included may local businessmen especially farmers and millers. Interest rates where stated were steady at 5% Sample voyages have been cited and I hop these were typical.

The overall trend of ship acquisition was a gradual build up to the 1840s and 50s when many cargo ships were built and owned locally, to a decline in the 1860s when second-hand ships were preferred and many of these especially at Cley and Blakeney were too big for coasting but cross traded. For example, North Norfolk ships could be found sailing out of London to the Meditrranean, or from Newcastle to the Baltic. After 1870, there is a steady downturn in the number of locally owned ships. The growth of the national railway system took away much traffic from the coasting trade and steamers did the same on the high seas. The depression in farming from the 1870s exacerbated matters. North Norfolk grain farmers found themselves in direct competition from cheap imports from the North American prairies, the Argentine and Australia. While Wells continued to be a commercial port to the end of the 20th century, Blakeney,Cley etc did not. That particular haven also suffered badly from silting too.

In the 19th century, all around the British Isles, there werc small ports with locally owned vessels, serving a predominantly rural hinterland, importing commodities such as coal and timber and exporting local produce such as minerals and grain. They played a role in a chain of distribution to and from the major ports. For example, London was linked to 580 places by water in 1800. Such small ports generated enough maritime trade to build up a fleet of ships to first supply the transport needs of the port and then to generate further income by tramping of developing special trades. In North Norfolk, for example, the basic traffic was coal in from the Humber or the North East and grain out to London or to the Humber. Other imports included timber and linseed cake from Hull, London or direct from the Baltic. Before the establishment of railways, there was also a general packet trade to London and Hull with fortnightly sailings. These might carry groceries and gods for local shops and the local aristocracy. The Cokes of Holkham for example sent turkeys down to their London house by sea. There was even a small amount of passenger traffic . In addition enterprising local shipowners bought bigger ships — some too big for their home ports — and went into tramp trades between other ports. Newcastle to the Baltic and London to the Mediterranean were the most popular choices.

A developing fleet also called for services: repairs, stores, crews etc and boosted local shore-side business. For example, the grocer and the draper might find they had a demand for ships' biscuits, salt meat, sea boots and oilskins. And so it was not surprising that many landlubbers in a port were prepared to invest some of their savings in local vessels. While a wooden sailing cargo ship carried many risks, on the whole most survived long enough to make a return but this was by no means guaranteed. Very few accounts survive from the coastal trade but as an example the firm of Mingay & Rope at Orford, Suffolk made a return of about 5% on their shipping activities. The total North Norfolk owned fleet averaged about 7000 tons between 1848 and 1876. It peaked at 9,500 tons in 1852. These totals included fishing boats that were registered. The small crab boats did not come in but the 'Great Boats' — 3 masted

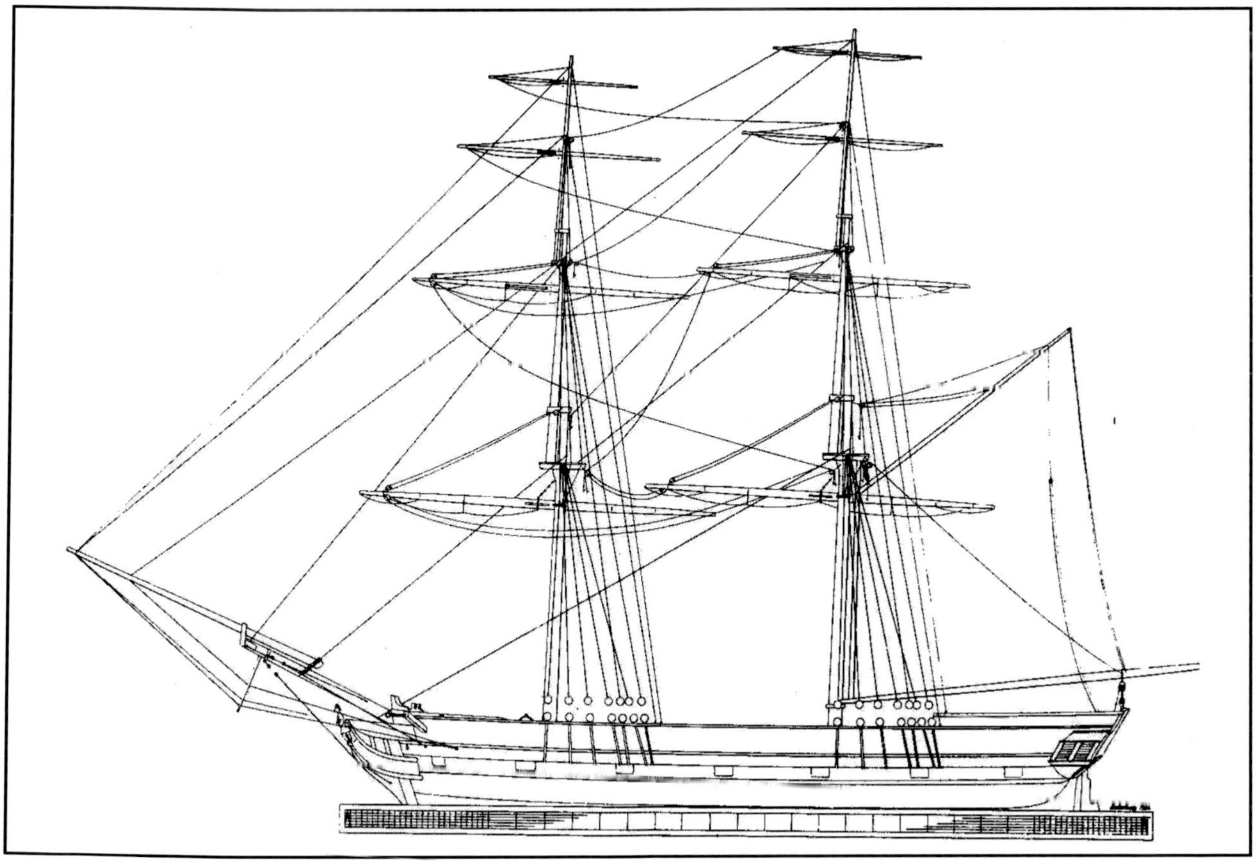

*Plan of the snow **BLACK PRINCE** 1838. A snow had an auxiliary mast behind the main mast. That was the only difference from a brig.*

Two-masted topsail schooner under sail. This un-named schooner in the Mersey gives a good impression of how most North Norfolk schooners were rigged.

luggers — mainly belonging to Sheringham did. A sample of cargo ships revealed that the average tonnage for a Wells-owned one was 78 tons and Cley/Blakeney 107. This was accounted for by the larger number of brigs etc owned in that latter ports. This was similar to other ports elsewhere.

The majority of vessels were rigged as 2-masted schooners, followed by single masted sloops. Many of the latter were billy-boys which had clinker and carvel hulls, and were fitted with leeboards, masts that could be lowered and running bowsprits which could be retracted. Fishing vessels were split between gaff-rigged smacks many of which had been transferred from other fishing ports and the luggers. Apart from the coaster ***Taffy*** owned by Page & Turner of Blakeney, only tugs steamers were ever owned in North Norfolk. I have included the paddle steamers which came to be stationed at Wells and Blakeney because they were so important to improving the safety and access to those ports.

I felt it would be useful at this point to set down my list of ships for others' use. It has accumulated over 50 years and has been used in various papers and a book on shipbuilding at Wells. I owe much thanks to many people. These include Bob Malster with whom I have corresponded over many years, Jonathon Hooton, the author of a splendid book on the Glaven ports, members of the Blakeney and District History Society and the Wells Local History Group, Adrian Osler who is an authority on the Newcastle–Baltic trade, David Cubitt an indefatigable researcher and a descendant of the Cubitts of Bacton, colleagues at Merseyside Maritime Museum, the late Tom Dack — direct descendant of the last shipwright at Wells, and Cecily and Roger, his daughter and son, and finally to my good friend Frank Large who helped me pull the whole manuscript together.

ABDIEL of Wells
98 tons, 58.9 ft, 18.6 ft, 10.9 ft, built at Sunderland 1827, snow. Master: Henry Gray.
SR 9/1848 & 8/1852 transferred from Whitby, Joseph Springall Southgate **64** shipowner of Wells.
Re-registered 1 June 1852 after alteration, revised tonnage 135 tons.
29 Sept 1889 no longer fit for sea.
Joseph Southgate was the foremost merchant and shipowner in Wells with many different business interests including owning one of the two shipyards and a local director of the Wells & Fakenham Railway. The latter venture cost him dearly. The ***ABDIEL*** was a typical Sunderland 'collier brig' – tubby (length to beam ratio of 1:3) and deep. Compare this with the Wells-built brig ***COUNTESS OF LEICESTER*** with a ratio 1:4. The alterations of 1852 must have been a major rebuilding given that she lasted until 1889. She does not appear in the sample sailings and arrivals of Wells and it could be that her extra draft meant that she traded elsewhere.

ABEONA of North Repps
26 tons, 47.2 ft, 13.6 ft, 6.3 ft, built at Lowestoft 1839, lugger, 3 masts, running bowsprit, clench build.
Master: Charles Symonds 1848, William Pardon 1850.
SR 11/1848 & 10/1850 Edmund Summers **64** carpenter of N Repps, 7 May 1850 sold to John Curtis farmer of N Repps.
23 Apr 1858 re-registered at Gt Yarmouth. This lugger was probably based at Cromer. Notice also how a local farmer became involved in shipowning.

ADELAIDE of Cley
76 tons. Master: R Parker [Lloyd's 1834].

ADMIRAL of Sheringham
25 tons, 45.6 ft, 13.8 ft, 6 ft 6 in, built 1842 by Lown & Lown, Sheringham, 3 masted lugger, running bowsprit, clench build. Master: Edmund Bayfield
SR10/1842 & 7/1846 Christopher West senior and junior and James West all fishermen of Sheringham **13** shares each, Edmund Bayfield **13** fisherman of Beeston, John Craske **6** fisherman of Beeston and Edmund West **6** fisherman of Sheringham. 11 May 1846 all other shareholders sold **51** shares to E Bayfield. 11 May 1847 E Bayfield sold **21** shares to Robert Nurse dealer of Weybourne, and **11** each to John Craske of Beeston and James Middleton of Sheringham both fishermen.
11 July 1862 re-registered at Gt Yarmouth.

ADRIEL of Sheringham
13 tons, 32 ft, 10.5 ft, 5.8 ft, built at Sheringham 1837, lugger, running bowsprit, clench build. Master: Benjamin Johnson.
SR 8/1846 & 8/1851 B Johnson and Joseph Nightingale **32** each, fishermen of Sheringham. 16 July 1851 all shares sold to John Harrison fisherman of Cromer.
25 Feb 1862 registry transferred to Gt Yarmouth.

ADVANCE of Wells
242 tons (rounded up), 85 ft 8 in, 25 ft 11 in, 15 ft, built at Sunderland 1825, brig, square stern. Master: Carter Balls.
SR 13/1833 James Chapman & George Crofts merchants, J H Parker & J S Southgate shipbuilders all of Wells **16** shares each. Mortgages 8 Feb 1834 Parker to Thomas Langton merchant, Lambeth Crofts to William Hewett merchant, Hull and 10 Oct 1834 Chapman **32** shares to Gurney, Birkbeck, bankers, Fakenham. At some unrecorded date Southgate must have sold his 16 shares to Chapman.
Fate 10 Oct 1835 sold to Newcastle owners and re-registered there.
All four were leading figures in the commerce of Wells. It looks as if this vessel (possibly damaged), which was large by Wells standard must have been jointly purchased with a view to selling her on.

AGAMEMNON of Wells
820 tons, 178.1 ft, 34.3 ft, 21 ft, built at Sunderland 1855, 3 masted ship, quarter gallery, figurehead removed at Liverpool and replaced with billet head 4 Oct 1865.
SR 8/1863 transferred from London Joseph Haycock shipowner of Wells. 29 Dec 1866 J Haycock sold **60** to William Jecks timber merchant of Beccles and **4** to Arnold George master mariner of Llys-y-Fran, Pembrokeshire. 24 Dec 1868 W Jecks sold **60** shares back to Joseph Haycock and 5 Oct 1870 he sold **21** on to Edward Pembroke shipbroker of London.
14 Oct 1872 abandoned off Cape Town.
The ***AGAMENON*** was the biggest ship ever registered at Wells and was far too big to trade with her home port. She was an ocean going tramp possibly in the timber trade while under Jeck's ownership. But Lloyd's Register of 1869 records she was bound from London to Madras and her abandonment off Cape Town also suggests she was a regular Indian trader. The purchase of a large ship such as the ***AGAMEMNON*** was not unique to Haycock or to Wells. Other shipowners in small ports did the same and used shipbrokers and agents in major ports to find charters for their vessels. There was probably more profit in deep sea trading than in coastal voyages. See ***CAROLINE*** for further details.

AGNES of Wells
71 tons, 59 ft 6 in, 16 ft 4 in, 7 ft 6 in, built 1834 by John Lubbock at Wells, sloop, running bowsprit, round stern.
Master: Robert Ringwood.
SR 1/1834 & 17/1836 Samuel Sharpe, merchant Brancaster. 12 Oct 1847 John Archibald of Thrapston, N'hants & William Brigant of N Creake gents and executors of late Sharpe of Docking sold all shares to John Byron shipowner, Hull.
Samuel Sharpe lived at Sunderland House Docking and may have farmed as well as working as a merchant. White's 1844 *Norfolk Directory* has a James Sharpe as a maltster, coal and corn merchant at Brancaster whose premises were down on the Quay. The ***AGNES***

is what might be termed a 'Norfolk billy-boy' since she was of the same hull proportions as the Humberside billy boys but was carvel built. 21 Jan 1843 she sailed from Wells with barley for Hull.

ALBION of Wells
50? tons, 56 ft 9 in, 14 ft 5 in, 5 ft 10 in, built at Walcot, Lincs. 1814, sloop, topping up bowsprit, round stern, clinker.
Masters: William Smith 1837, Thomas Harrison 31 Apr 1837, William Smith 5 Oct 1838, William Cook 13 Feb 1839, John Cooper 3 Feb 1840, William Smith, Francis Oliver Cooper 31 Oct 1843, 23 Mar 1845 John Oliver Cooper, 3 May 1845 Thomas Nicholls.
SR 1/1834, 14/1836, 2/1843 George Crofts, merchant, Wells **64** shares. 11 Feb 1834 mortgaged John Woodley, corn factor of Crutched Friars, London. 5 June 1840 mortgage discharged and 14 ? 1842 sold her to Joseph Haycock, the Younger, merchant of London. 8 Oct 1842 re-registered at London 305/1842. 2/1843 at Wells James Chapman merchant **64**, 22 Jan 1845 Chapman sold **64** to John Lubbock, shipbuilder of Wells.
22 Feb 1848 broken up.
John Woodley was a major dealer in East Anglian grain on the London Cornmarket. James Chapman was a leading coal and corn merchant, and was one of the investor's in Wells' first steam tug (the ***ECONOMY*** 1/1840). The ***ALBION*** was a proper clinker-built billy boy. See ***CAROLINE*** for more detail on Haycocks.

ALBION of Cromer
59 tons, 57.8 ft, 15.4 ft, 8.3 ft, built 1819 at Cley, schooner. Master: William Payne 1843.
SR 8/1843 John William Rust grocer & draper **32** and William Rigden master mariner both of Cromer. 1852 broken up. Rigden had **32** shares in the ***COMMERCE*** and by 1853 he was listed as a shipowner at Middleborough see ***CATHERINE***. Cromer was growing a seaside resort even before the arrival of the railway in 1877. It had doubled its population between 1801 and 1841. According to White's 1844 Norfolk Directory '*... it enjoys some little trade, in the importation of coals, tiles, oil cake, porter etc in vessels of from 60 to 100 tons.*' Curiously John Rust was listed as a farmer while a Benjamin Rust was one of the 8 grocers in the town. No doubt, the Rusts had supplies of imported foods and textiles carried from London in the ***ALBION***.

ALBION of Wells
69 tons, 57.9 ft, 15.9 ft, 8.9 ft, built at Wells 1827, brigantine.
Masters: John Hayden, William Cringle, Hammond Thomas Abbs 1852, 4 June 1857 Robert Thomas.
SR 1/1827, 18/1836, 3/1846 & 2/1852 Original shareholders unknown as Registers only survive from 1832. 13 June 1835 Susan Crofts widow of Fakenham mortgaged **22** shares to William Sheringham, gent. of Fakenham, to secure £900 + interest. 21 May 1836 Joshua Gates grocer of Wells **42** and Susan Crofts **22**. 14 Feb 1846 Sheringham sold **22** to Rev. John Drake Crofts of Little Walsingham for £150 free of encumbrances of late Susan Crofts deceased. He was curate to Rev. H J Lee-Warner and also appointed a Wells Harbour Commissioner in 1835 [Purchas 1965: 61]. 12 Mar 1852 Gates sold **21** shares to Hammond Thomas Abbs, mariner of Runton and David Vial carpenter of Cromer [also lodging house keeper according to White's 1844 *Norfolk Directory*], 8 June 1853 executors of Crofts sold his **22** shares to Vial and 9 Sept 1853 Vial now listed as a farmer sold **11** shares to Abbs.
With her transfer to Cromer and Runton owners, it is likely that she was working off the beach at these places. Vial's different occupations – carpenter, lodging house keeper, farmer and shipowner – was common for enterprising small 19th century businessmen. Nor was it uncommon for grocers to be involved in owning shares. It is likely that the management of the ship would left to the Abbs the master and shareholder. The ***ALBION*** is very small for a square rigged vessel.

ALBION of Wells
47 tons 59.5 ft, 15.4 ft, 7.3 ft, built at Southwick, Lincs 1838, sloop (schooner after 1881) round stern, carvel & clench build.
SR 10/1858 transferred from Boston Thomas Lord coal merchant (and farmer according to Harman) of Wells **64**. 1Mar 1879 T Lord sold **32** to William B Smith, shipping agent of Gaywood near King's Lynn and **32** to James Smith junior master mariner of Wells.
19 Dec 1879 co-owners sell **64** to Samuel Deveson, shipbuilder of Ramsgate and re-registered at Ramsgate.
The quick sale to a shipbuilder might suggest that she needed costly repairs. The place of build is a puzzle because there is no Southwick in Lincolnshire. But given her build, she was almost certainly from that area. An alternative might be Stockwith near Gainsborough on the River Trent.

ALERT of Cley
198 tons, 94.3 ft, 25.4 ft, 14.2 ft, foreign built, condemned by the Court of Admiralty 25 Apr 1857, brig converted to a brigantine 26 Jan 1874, billet head.
SR 6/1860 Robert Henry Cooper 64 shipowner of Wiveton.
8 Sept 1880 **64** sold to George Henry Collins merchant of Dartmouth and John Ellis farmer of Kingswear, transferred to Dartmouth Registry. I suspect shipowner may cover some other occupation such as farmer.

ALERT of Blakeney
21 tons, 43.7 ft, 14.9 ft, 6.5 ft, built at Ipswich 1861, smack.
SR 9/1866 19 Nov 1866 Robert Vince **64** shipowner of Blakeney. 8-9 Feb 1867 R Vince sold **4** shares to each of the following Charles Johnson Temple, shipowner, William Baker postmaster, James Parker, Felix Ransome, James Dew and James Woodhouse master mariners and Susanna Boyce milliner all of Blakeney. 4 July 1871 all other owners sold their shares to R Vince. 5 July 1871 R Vince sold **64** to George Able shipowner of King's Lynn. 21 Sept 1874 G Able sold **64** to Joseph Henry Dew fisherman of King's Lynn and 6 Jan 1879 J H Dew mortgaged **64** to William Brisco Whall accountant of King's Lynn in security of £35 + interest. 1 Mar 1880 mortgage discharged.
4 Dec 1884 J H Dew sold **64** to John Garner fisherman of Dunston Ferry, Lincs. Registry changed to Hull.
It is puzzling why so many investors were recruited for a fishing boat.

ALFRED of Wells
70 tons 61 ft 15.8 ft 8.7 ft, built at Gt Yarmouth 1806, brigantine. Masters: John Curson, 26 June 1846 John Hudson.
SR 38/1825 & 6/1836 John Curson **48** and Robert Chadd **16** master mariners both of Wells. 24 Feb 1846 both owners sell **32** shares to John Hudson master mariner of Wells.
1 July 1853 registry closed vessel missing since 12 Dec 1852.
Voyages included 18 Jan 1845 arr Wells in ballast from Maldon, 23 Feb & 23 Nov 1850 sailed for Hartlepool in ballast, 29 June & 30 Nov 1850 arrived from Hartlepool with coal. Over 1850-51 the ***ALFRED*** seems to have specialised in coal cargoes from Hartlepool.

ALGERINA of Wells
65 tons, 57.8 ft, 15.8 ft, 8.7 ft, built at Wells 1805 sloop, running bowsprit. Master: 1834 Bocking, 1836 Joseph Dix.
SR 11/1836 Samuel Sharpe merchant Sunderland House, Docking **64**. 18 Apr 1836 **32** shares sold to John Harrison publican of the Le Strange Arms, Hunstanton and **16** to Thomas Ulph publican of Titchwell.
20 Apr 1836 registry transferred to King's Lynn.
See also ***AGNES*** and ***ANN***.

ALNWICK CASTLE of Blakeney
55 tons, 58.5 ft, 15.4 ft, 8.3 ft, built 1842 at Aberdeen. Master: 1848 Butcher Starling.
SR 7/1848 transferred from Berwick. John Starling **64** merchant of Blakeney (Whites's 1864 *Norfolk Directory* John Starling listed also as a farmer and a miller). 23 May 1848 J Starling sold **20** to John Sayer gent of Field Dalling (farmer in White 1844).
31 Mar 1854 Starling and Sayer sell **64** shares to Duncan Livingston mariner of Plockton, Rosshire.
John Starling owned 9 ships between 1843 and 1864 and employed relatives such as Butcher to command them. In 1850 this vessel was engaged in the carrying coal from Newcastle 23 Feb, 2 Mar, 30 Mar 1850.

ALSWOLD of Sunderland
300 tons, built 1866 at S Hylton, Sunderland, Official No. 47685.
Owned by William Allen of Weybourne [Mercantile Navy List 1872-77 & Mills, 1957:130 painting of ***ALSWOLD***]

AMARATH of Wells
110 tons, 72.2 ft, 21.8 ft, 10.8 ft, built at Sunderland in 1848, brig.
SR 3/1866 Richard Cawdron Smith pilot **4**, James Elenor Smith shipwright **3**, Hammond John Parker master mariner **3**, Robert Plattin painter **6**, Robert Oldham master mariner **8**, Edward John Matson boatman **2**, John Plumb Ramm innkeeper **4**, John Ramm boatman **5**, Edward Wordingham master mariner **2**, Francis B Southgate, shipowner **4**, John Shreeve shipwright **8**, Jon Cringle master mariner **2**, Edward Bailey Baines **6**, William Green painter **4**, Henry Byfield Fryer stationer **3**. All of Wells.
23 Mar 1867 lost on Happisburgh Sands.
It was unusual to have as many as 15 shareholders for one North Norfolk vessel though it was common elsewhere e.g. North Wales. It is unclear what the connection was between them: seven were seamen and two were shipwrights. Francis Southgate concealed his main occupation which was the postmaster in Staithe Street, John Ramm was landlord of the *Jolly Sailors* in the East End and John Shreeve was the landlord and a brewer as well as a shipwright at the *Red Lion* on the Quay.

ANN of Wells
94 tons, 68.3 ft, 16.4 ft, 9.3 ft, built at Wells 1804, brigantine. Masters: William Newson, 13 June 1837 James Brereton.
SR 1/1836 Robert Leeder senior, shipowner, Robert Leeder junior victualler, William Newsom mariner and Robert London master mariner all of Wells with **16** shares each. 12 June 1837 all the above sell **32** shares to James Neave shipowner and **16** to Robert Shingle Watling agent, both of Great Yarmouth and **16** to John Crisp junior corn merchant of Beccles.
6 Sept 1836 registry transferred to Yarmouth.
J & R Brereton was a noted merchants and shipowners at Wells and Blakeney. Robert Leeder senior was the landlord of the *Sun*, Wells, 1812 to 1839 and his son took over in 1839 and continued until 1865 [Welland, 2012: 73]. Robert Neave lived at St. George's Terrace, Yarmouth and John Crisp junior was a coal and corn merchant and shipowner at Northgate St., Beccles.

ANN of Wells
23 tons 34 ft 10 in, 12 ft 10 in, 6 ft 3 in, built at Wells 1830, sloop, running bowsprit. Master: Christopher Cook.
SR 8/1830, 5/1838 & 1/1848 Samuel Castle **64** gardener of Wells. 21 Apr 1840 mortgaged to Robert Leeder, innkeeper of Wells, discharged 4 Nov 1845, and same day sold to Thomas Bunn master mariner of Wells.
26 Feb 1848 T Bunn sold **64** to William Coker merchant of Wells.
26 Feb 1853 W Coker sold **64** to John Magnus fisherman of Wells (bill of sale 5 Sept 1851).

ANN of Wells
74 tons 61 ft 1 in, 16 ft 7 in, 9 ft 2 in, built at Wells 1809, brigantine. Master: William Dickings.
SR 8/1826 & 5/1836 Samuel Sharpe merchant of Sunderland House, Docking **64**.
9 Sept 1847 re-registered at King's Lynn.
Sharpe was also owner of the ***AGNES***. Sunderland Farm is at the north end of Docking parish and lies some 3 miles to the south of Brancaster OS TG784395.

ANN of Cley
126 tons, 68 ft, 21 ft, 12 ft 3 in, built at Peterhead 1830, snow, female bust figurehead.
Masters: Francis Mussett, Francis Plumb 1841-1844.
SR 8/1839 Thomas Beckwith clerk **32**, Marjorie Moore widow **16**, John Copeman butcher **8**, Phebe Digby (wife of John Digby

shoemaker) **8** all of Cley. 22 Mar 1842 P Digby sold **8** shares to F Plumb, master mariner of Blakeney. 20 Feb 1844 Plumb sold his **8** shares to Robert Mann, master mariner of Cley.
Thomas Beckwith was curate of Wiveton church. In White's 1844 *Norfolk Directory*, there was a Margaret Moore who may be the same as the Marjorie listed. The combination of two women, a clergyman and a butcher as shareholders was unusual. It would be nice to know if Marjorie (Margaret) was responsible for managing the ship. She also had shares in the ***DUKE OF WELLINGTON*** and ***WILLIAM IV*** along with Thomas Beckwith. There is a watercolour painting of the ***ANN*** by H J Hansen of Altona dated 1841. She certainly traded between London and Hamburg [Hooton, 2003: 17-18]. It is that she was the ***ANN*** reported at Cley in the *Norfolk News* for 29 Sept 1845 from Dantzig with a cargo of oil seed cake.

ANN of Blakeney
109 tons, 64.7 ft, 16.8 ft, 10.6 ft, built at Wells by John Lubbock 1840, schooner, female bust. Master: Edward Ferris Wallis.
SR 14/1840 Robert J Brereton & Randle J Brereton merchants of Blakeney **32** shares each. 16/1856 Randle Brereton **64**. 7 Feb 1860 **64** shares mortgaged to Harvey & Co, Bankers of Norwich on £2000 + interest. 15 Jan 1863 Harvey & Co sell **64** to R. Cubitt merchant of Wells. 9 Dec 1874 R Cubitt died **64** shares to his executor Augustus Hill, farmer on behalf of his widow Harriett.
9 Apr 1878 wrecked near Scarborough.
The Breretons were maltsters and shipowners at Blakeney. In all they had shares in ten ships between 1840 and 1860. In the latter year his fleet of six ships were mortgaged to Harveys for a total of £2000. As Harvey sold them on to other owners, the inference must be that Randle had gone bankrupt. Such were the risks of the shipping business.

ANN of Blakeney
291 tons, 97 ft, 26.3 ft, 17.2 ft, built at Sunderland 1845, brig, female figurehead.
SR 1/1859 transferred from London Thomas William Temple **64** merchant of Blakeney. 19 Jan 1859 T W Temple sold **8** to William Patrick, butcher of Newcastle, **7** to Charles Temple merchant of Blakeney, **22** to William Farquaher chronometer maker of King St, Tower Hill, London. 16 May 1859 T W Temple sold **22** to David Thomas master mariner of Blakeney.
28 June 1865 all shares sold to Hamburg owners.
Charles and William Temple were in business as maltsters. Between 1839 and 1877 they owned 12 ships. Six were small coasters and six of over 100 tons including the barque ***SAMUEL ENDERBY*** of 403 tons. They seem to have had a policy of selling on most of the shares while retaining the managing ownership. William and Charles only had **12** in the ***ANN***. She was a large ship for Blakeney and the chances are that she was on European routes and not in the local coastal trade.

ANNE of Overstrand
50 tons, 45 ft, 15.8 ft, 9.7 ft, built at Allen (probably Alloa on the Forth), Scotland, 1819, sloop, running bowsprit.
Master: James Harrison.
SR 9/1842 Jeremiah Cross 64 merchant of Overstrand. 7 July 1849 registry cancelled, broken up.
Jeremiah Cross was also a farmer who probably used the ***ANNE*** to deliver coal and take away grain from the beach at Overstrand. Given the costs of road transport and the North Walsham & Dilham Canal, landing cargoes on beaches remained the best method of bulk transport for coastal voyages. It was inherently dangerous and trade would be suspended in winter.

ANNIE of Wells or Blakeney
30 ton fishing smack 4 crew, Official No. 65818, transferred from Grimsby to King's Lynn 5/1887.

ANN & MARIA
79 tons, 60 ft, 17 ft, 9.6 ft, built at Wells 1840, schooner, woman's bust figurehead. Master: Thomas Southerland
SR 7/1855 Martin Dodman 64 merchant of Titchwell. 17 Feb 1855 executors of M Dodman Senior Martin Dodman Junior merchant and Alfred Dodman civil engineer transfer **64** shares to M Dodman Junior.
24 July 1864 M Dodman sold **64** shares to George Palmer, shipowner of Boston.
The Dodmans were farmers at Titchwell and it is likely that their schooner traded out of Brancaster or Thornham. Alfred Dodman was the engineer who founded the famous firm of agricultural and steam engineers at King's Lynn in 1850.

ARIEL of Blakeney
90 tons, 63.3 ft, 18.4 ft 11.1 ft, built at Rye by James Hessell 1840, schooner, lute stern, female bust figurehead (removed 1861 and gammon knee instead). Master: John Smithers, Robert Howes 1865-1879
SR 19/1840 Charles Temple merchant **16**, Thomas Haren master mariner **16**, Charles Buck , John Smithers **8**, Hannah Nurse (wife of William Ward Nurse) **8**, all of Blakeney, Charles Buck surgeon of Cley **18** and William Purdy gent of Witchingham **8**. 23 July 1850 John Smithers sold **8** to William Isaac Bensley master mariner of Blakeney. SR 2/1859 10 Mar 1859 sold to Richard Howes **32**, Mikes Lane **16**, William Allen Lane **16** all master mariners of Blakeney. SR 2/1865 Richard Howes 64 master mariner of Blakeney. 2 Apr 1876 R Howes mortgaged **64** to W B S G Buxton banker of Fakenham to secure £140 + interest. 30 May 1878 R Howes took a second mortgage with Thomas Cook merchant of King's Lynn for £70 + interest. 9 Sept 1878 this second mortgage discharged.
9 May 1879 R Howes sold **64** to Lewis Beckett Cooper retired merchant of Lowestoft. Registry transferred to Lowestoft.
Charles Temple and his relative Thomas William Temple were maltsters who owned twelve ships between 1839 and 1864. Their policy as with the ***ARIEL*** was to hold a small number of shares (usually twelve to sixteen) and sell the remainder. Their masters usually took some but the mix of investors in the case of the ***ARIEL*** is intriguing. One expects master mariners and even their wives but what persuaded a doctor and a gentleman to make such an investment?
Robert Howes was a master/owner whose finances forced him into taking out loans. Country bankers (in this case Gurneys) were often reluctant to lend money against the security of a ship but the branch manager at Fakenham seemed to have been more sympathetic than most.

ARGUS of Brancaster
42 tons, built 1839. Master & owner H Skipper.
Registered at King's Lynn and listed in Clayton's Shipping Register 1865.

ARK of Sheringham
11 tons, 32.3 ft, 10 ft, 5 ft, built 1838 at Sheringham, 3 masted lugger, running bowsprit, clench build.
Master: William Johnson.
SR 6/1842 & 12/1848 John and Richard Cox **32** shares each, fishermen of Sheringham. 14 June 1848 the Coxes sold **22** to William Johnson, **21** each to Matthew and Robert Johnson all fishermen of Sheringham.
1870 registry closed under 15 tons.

ARROW of Cley
103 tons, 64.8 ft, 18.4 ft, 11 ft, built at Sunderland 1841, schooner.
Master: James Randall, George Purser 25 Oct 1852, James Randall 3 Dec 1852.
SR 9/1841 John Ebbetts gent **11**, John Randall mariner **6**, Edward Sturges bricklayer **9**, William Gabb mariner **6**, Catherine Dingle widow **4**, all of Cley, William Thomas Smith shipowner (in fact Grocer and draper) **1**, Clarke Painter shipowner (plumber & glazier) **6** of Holt, Thomas Lubbock farm bailiff **9** and Thomas Lynes gardener **9** of Kelling. 20 Nov 1844 E Sturges sold **9** to J Ebbetts now of Gt Witchingham. 13 Feb 1849 C Painter sold **4** to George Pattison Dingle gent of E Dereham. 16 Nov 1850 E Ebbetts widow & executrix to J Ebbetts and executors John E Ebbets farmerof Colton, Edward Juby farmer of Beeston and Edward Bird farmer of Cawston sold **7** to C Painter. 30 Nov 1850 T H Smith sold **2** to C Painter (he must have bought another one which is not recorded in the main Register). 3 May 1851 Ann Dingle widow and Robert Cooper solicitor of E Dereham executors for G P Dingle sold **4** to Thomas Osborne Springfield gent of Norwich.
6 April 1863 sold and re-registered at Ipswich.
Yet again, a miscellany of investors who presumably received a decent return since most retained their shares for 22 years. As the ***ARROW*** was bought as a new vessel, her likely building price was about £7.00 a ton, a total of £721 which made each share £11.26. This was not an inconsiderable sum in 1841 given the risky nature of the investment. Clearly Blakeney and Cley vessels offered sufficient returns for all these landsmen and women to place their capital in ships.

BEAR PARK of Cley
96 tons, 60 ft, 20 ft, 10.5 ft, built at Sunderland 1835, schooner. Master: Jeremiah Moore.
WSR 8/1841 Robert Nash **64** farmer of Salthouse. 27 Apr 1847 registry cancelled, wrecked Oct 1846. Salthouse is the next coastal parish to Cley. It had a channel connected to the Glaven estuary in 16th century [Hooton, 1996: 109]. The **BEAR PARK** probably delivered cargoes to Cley. **BEAR PARK** may be a surname rather than a location.

BESSEY of Brancaster
37 tons?, 57.4 ft, 15 ft, 6 ft, built Knottingley 1826, sloop, round stern, carvel & clench built.
Master: Samuel Powditch 1850, James High 1857.
WSR 4/1850 & 2/1857 16 Feb 1857 transferred from Goole, Samuel Powditch **64** master mariner of Brancaster. 16 Feb 1857 James High **32** master mariner of Brancaster, Robert Jackson **32** shepherd of Warham.
26 Jan 1862 R Jackson left **32** to his widow Rebecca and 26 Mar 1863 she sold **32** to James High junior.
18 Apr 1863 J High jun sold **32** to Womack shipbuilder of Stanley Ferry, Wakefield.
This another example of a billy boy, useful tonnage and draught for regularly trading to and from Brancaster.

BETSY of Wells
13 tons, 30.6 ft, 10 ft, 3.5 ft built at Ipswich 1784, smack, running bowsprit.
Master: Robert Crofford **64** master mariner of Wells.
27 Oct 1855 broken up.
Probably used for fishing given her tonnage. Many masters turned to fishing as a living in old age.

BETSY of Wells
56 tons, 55.5 ft 15.1 ft, 7.6 ft, built 1841 by John Lubbock at Wells, sloop, round stern, running bowsprit.
Master: John Mussett 1841.
WSR 11/1841 Samuel Sharpe **64** merchant (and farmer) Sunderland House, Docking.
1 Apr 1847 executors of S Sharpe sold **64** to James Mann of Boston, re-registered at Boston.
She was a Norfolk version of the billy boy with a carvel hull, same proportions and rig. Sharpe was the sole shareholder of 5 ships: **BETSY**, **LUCY**, **ANN**, **ALGERINA** and **AGNES**. On 11 Jan. 1845 the **BETSY** sailed from Wells with a cargo of barley for Hull.

BLAKENEY of Cley
151 tons, brig? J Portermaster [Lloyds 1834]

BLACKNEY of Blakeney
88 tons, 66.5 ft, 18.6 ft 10.4 ft, built 1814 at Southtown, Gt Yarmouth, brigantine. Master: W Harvey 1857.
WSR 8/1857 (from Sunderland) Randle Brereton **64** merchant Blakeney. 6 Feb 1860 **64** shares mortgaged to Harvey & Co bankers of Norwich as part of security on £2000+interest. 21 Jan 1862 Harveys sold **32** each to Thomas and John Powditch shipowners of Wells.
5 Nov 1864 lost on Eccles beach (Norfolk).
Randle was in partnership with Robert John Brereton. They were major merchant and shipowners in Blakeney but got into financial difficulties and all 4 of their ships were mortgaged and then sold off by their bankers. Provincial bankers were usually very wary about lending money on the security of ships.

The ANNE of Goole was a good example of how a billy-boy such as CONCORD of Wells would have been rigged with a square topsail and topgallant sail.

BLACK-EYED SUSAN of Wells or Blakeney
24 ton fishing smack, 4 crew, Official No. 8210, King's Lynn registry 7/1887.

BLAKENEY AND HULL PACKET of Blakeney
35.5 tons, 58 ft, 15.8 ft, 5.9 ft, built 1832 at Wells, sloop, round stern.
Master: Kitwood 1834, James Hamm 1854, William Allen 1869.
WSR 8/1854, 13/1856 & 1/1869 Randle & Robert Brereton each **32** merchants of Blakeney. 22 Oct 1856 re-registered. 26 Jan 1860 64 shares in Randle's name were mortgaged to Harvey & Co bankers of Norwich as part security on £2000+5% interest. 16 Jan 1863 Harvey & Co sold 64 to John Savory gent (White's 1864 Norfolk Directory miller, maltster & merchant of Burnham Overy and Richard Parker merchant of Wells. 30 Mar 1869 J Savory & R Parker sell **64** shares to William Allen master mariner of King's Lynn. 24 Sept 1873 W Allen **32** each to George Balding senior shipwright of Blakeney and Robert Balding innkeeper of Dersingham.
9 Dec 1874 wrecked at Whitby.
Her name suggests she was on a regular run between Blakeney and Hull probably delivering grain and returning with parcels of groceries, Baltic timber and linseed cake. She sailed for Hull on 30 Mar 1850.

BLAKENEY PACKET of Cley
57 tons. Master: Bainbridge [Lloyds 1834]

BLAKENEY of Cley
64 tons. Master: J Hurn [Lloyds 1834]

BLAKENEY TRADER of Blakeney
67 tons, 61 ft, 18 ft, 9 ft, built 1826 at Blakeney, schooner. Master: J Bowls 1834.
WSR 9/1856 8 Sept 1856 Randle Brereton **64**. 6 Feb 1860 **64** mortgaged to Harvey & Co bankers of Norwich as part of security for a loan of £2000+ 5% interest.
4 July 1862 lost off Redcar on passage from Newcastle (probably with coal) to St Valery. Five of the crew were saved.
The Breretons seem to have managed to hold on to this vessel whereas the **BLACKNEY** and others were sold off. Redcar is just to the south of the River Tees. St Valery could be either St Valery-en-Caux or St Valery-sur-Somme both in Normandy. This shows the kind of cross trading that North Norfolk vessels engaged in.

BLUE JACKET of Blakeney
57 tons, 62.5 ft, 17.4 ft, 7.8 ft, built 1860 at Walsoken, ketch. Master: Samuel Jary in 1890s [Hooton 1996: 251]
WSR 2/1868 27 Feb 1868 transferred from Wisbech: Benjamin Henry Nichols **64** shipowner and merchant of Blakeney. 24 Jan 1878

mortgaged to Gurney's Bank, Fakenham for loan of £450+ 5% interest, discharged 20 Sept 1878. Same day B H Nicholls sold **64** to Martin Fountain Page merchant of Blakeney. 22 July 1882 M F Page sold **64** to aforesaid MFP and Edward Clifford Turner as Page & Turner merchants and shipowners of Blakeney. 7 Sept 1896 Page & Turner sold **64** E C Turner. 11 Mar 1908 E C Turner sold **64** to ECT, Ellis Capps Turner & Alfred Edward Turner merchants and shipowners of Blakeney.
15 Apr 1911 converted into a houseboat.
Walsoken lies on the outskirts of Wisbech on the River Nene. Page & Turner were the main merchants at Blakeney with other premises at Cley and Holt railway station. Kelly's 1896 *Norfolk Directory* describes them as corn, coal, cake (oilseed), seed and manure merchants. They owned several other ships including the **TAFFY**, a small steam coaster. The **BLUE JACKET** was a large carvel-built version of the billy-boy and was first rigged with a square topsail and topgallant on her main mast. After major hull damage in 1887, these yards were removed. She became a dumb lighter in 1909 for work between the Pit anchorage and Blakeney Quay but was too big. In 1911, she became a houseboat embedded in the salt marsh near Morston. Her remains were recorded by Peter Catling who also made a model of her [Catling, 1965: 17-18 & 23]. She was named after a late 18th century Shawnee chief. His name was adopted for various ships including a famous American clipper of 1854.

BRISK of Wells or Blakeney
20 ton fishing smack, 2 crew, Official No. 53000, King's Lynn Registry 4/1881.

BRITISH QUEEN of Brancaster
15 tons 35.8 ft 11.4 ft, 6.1 ft, built 1823 at Cowes cutter, running bowsprit, clench build. A former revenue cutter.
WSR 3/1848 22 Apr 1848 William Allen **64** fisherman and skipper of Brancaster.
4 Jan 1858 broken up.

BROTHERS of Wells or Blakney
27 ton fishing smack 4 crew, Official No. 58618, Lynn registry 4/1887, closed 24 Dec 1897 vessel unseaworthy.

BRUNO of Brancaster
16 tons, 31 ft 4 in, 11 ft 9 in, 5 ft 10 in, built 1814 at King's Lynn, smack, runnning bowsprit, clench build.
WSR 2/1848 Joseph Dowdy **64** fisherman and skipper of Brancaster.
5 July 1849 J Dowdy sold **64** to John Mussett fisherman of Brancaster. Re-registered 8/1949
27 Dec 1864 broken up.

BUOY YACHT
73 tons, 58.1 ft, 16.2 ft, 10.2 ft, built at Rotherhithe 1791, schooner. Master: John Hudson 1842 and later John Hudson junior.
WSR 1/1842 5 Mar 1842 John Hudson **48** and John junior **16** both mariners of Wells. 5 Mar 1847 Hudson senior sold **16** to Hudson junior. 2 May 1853 William Segar executor (and grocer and draper) of Wells sold deceased senior's **32** to John Curson coal merchant of Wells.
20 May 1853 sold and re-registered at Lowestoft and still sailing out of Lowestoft 1865 [Clayton].
This vessel was presumably built by Trinity House as a buoy tender and as such was strongly built. This borne out by the fact she was still working in 1865 after 74 years service.
5 Apr 1845 she arrived at Wells from London and left for Newcastle on 3 May. In 1850, she seems to have been a regular run in ballast to Hartlepool to pick up coal.

BUXTON of Sheringham
15 tons, built 1834 at Sheringham, lugger?
WSR 7/1841 Henry Nockless **64** fisherman and skipper of Cromer.
25 Jan 1861 registry cancelled as under 15 tons.

CALTHORPE of Blakeney
70 tons, 61.5 ft, 17.2 ft, 9 ft, built 1817 at Wells, Official No. 22433, schooner, running bowsprit.
Master: 1845 William Bensley (see **CHARLEMAGNE** etc), 1865 J Woodhouse [Clayton].
Cley Reg 2/ 1836, WSR 4/1845 Charles Temple **32** merchant and Mrs Mary Temple **32** both of Blakeney. Date? Thomas William Temple & Charles Temple executors of late Mrs M Temple inherit her **32** shares.
1873 registry cancelled, converted into lighter at Blakeney.
Deeper draft ships partly discharged their cargoes for Blakeney and Cley in the Pit anchorage. The Temples were maltsters as wells a shipowners and owned shares in twelve vessels between 1839 and 1864 including coasters and deep sea ships e.g **SQUIRREL** 1839 or **SAMUEL ENDERBY** of 1858. The **CALTHORPE** was a regular coal run from Newcastle to Blakeney in 1850.

CAMELLIA of Blakeney
72 tons, 67.5 ft, 18.2 ft, 8.55 ft, built 1838 place unknown schooner.
WSR 3/1861 Charles Temple **32** merchant (& maltster) and Samuel Daniel **16** master mariner (possibly master) both of Blakeney and Hannah & Elizabeth Bolding spinsters of Weybourne **8** each. 15 Sept 1876 C Temple sold **32** to Charles Johnson Turner merchant of Blakeney.
10 Apr 1881 wrecked on Blakeney Sands.
Charles and Thomas Temple had shares in some 15 ships between 1839 and 1876. They were the managing owners who sold off a high proportion of the 64 shares. They bought small old ships (**SQUIRREL** 1839) commissioned new ships (**ENTEPRISE** 1840) and large second hand ships (**SAMUEL ENDERBY** 1858). The Bolding family owned a maltings, brewery and water mill in Weybourne. Hannah and Esther were sisters whose brother William took over the family business on his father's decease in 1847.

He was also a talented artist and pioneer photographer. It is puzzling to find Esther listed as a spinster because she married William Monement of King's Lynn in 1845 [Jefferson, 2003: 3-14]. The *Norfolk Chronicle* for 12 Jan 1850 reported her sailing for Newcastle.

CAROLINE of Wells
127 tons, 69 ft, 18.1 ft, 12.1 ft, built 9 Jan 1845 by John Lubbock at Wells, schooner, woman's bust.
Master: John Cademy 1845-53.
WSR 3/1845, 10/1845 & 11/1845 Joseph Haycock junr. **64** merchant of Wells. 8 Dec 1845 assigned to George John Graham & Emmanuel Cooper assignees of Joseph Haycock bankrupt who sold **64** to Abraham Dunn merchant of Wells. 8 Dec 1845 A Dunn sold **64** back to J Haycock. 9 Dec 1845 J Haycock mortgaged **64** to John Savory miller of Burnham Overy for security on £1500+ 5% interest. 17 Dec 1846 vessel also mortgaged to Major, Usborne & Kerr corn factors of London.
31 Jan 1855 re-registered, eventual fate?
Joseph Haycock senior was a merchant of Wells while his son was a merchant in London. The directories do not differentiate between the two. Joseph junior moved back to Wells and his father moved to London in 1845 (see **HUNTSMAN**). He clearly had difficulty in paying for his new schooner and was bankrupt until he could raise the necessary loan. Joseph junior was 28 at the 1851 Census with a wife and 6 small children and 3 servants. Helen aged 6 had been born in Lewisham in 1845 and Sidney aged 5 had been born in Wells in 1846 which suggests the family moved there in 1845. *Norfolk News* for 13 September 1851 advertised the auction of his house and granaries on the Quay. Directories for 1854 and 1856 still give his address as the Quay but White's 1864 edition stated that his house was in Staithe Street and his business premises on the Quay. Haycock was probably a Quaker because in 1861 his uncle George Haycock, a Quaker of Chelmsford, left his children £43,000 in trust until they reached 23. He was involved with the local branch of the Oddfellows Friendly Society and a shareholder in the Wells & Fakenham Railway and a public benefactor in 1859 when he and lawyer Hugh Rump paid for a clock on the church tower. Besides the **CAROLINE**, he owned the **LITTLE HELEN** and **SIDNEY CLAUDE** named after two of his children, **ENVOY, GLEANER, PEARL, ORKNEY LASS, CONCORD** and **AGAMENON**. Joseph senior had shares in the **INDUSTRY, HUNTSMAN** and **ALBION**.

CAROLINUS of Blakeney
42 tons, billy-boy? 3 crew, Official No. 67355, King's Lynn registry 13/1882.
1883 converted to a lighter.

CATHERINE of Cromer
48 tons, 43.9 ft, 15 ft, 8.5 ft, built 1841 at Newburgh (2 coastal Newburghs in Scotland in Fife and Aberdeen), schooner, 1 deck and break. Master: William Payne.
WSR 1/1853 5 Feb 1853 (transferred from London) William Rigden **22** shipowner (previously master mariner of Cromer – see **ALBION** and **COMMERCE**), Middlesborough, Henry Wright **21** merchant [also farmer see White's 1844 *Norfolk Directory*] of Runton and William Payne **21** master mariner of Cromer.
5 May 1859 **64** sold to John Middleton of London, transferred to Faversham Register.

CHANCE of Mundesley
70 tons, 60 ft, 16.4 ft, 8.5 ft, built 1798 at Gt Yarmouth, schooner. Master: William Kirk.
WSR 3/1850 (transferred from Gt Yarmouth) 9 Feb 1850 John Kirk **21** farmer. William Kirk **21** master mariner and Thomas Woodhouse **22** coal merchant all of Mundesley
10 Apr 1850 vessel lost.
An unlucky venture. Ships regularly beached at Mundesley to discharge and load as seen in the charges levied in 1856: £1 10s for pilotage (inc. ropes and baskets), discharging coal 13 men must be employed 1.5d per chaldron and 1 pint of beer per 10 chaldrons, cartage 1s 3d per chaldron, timber and deals 13 men at 5s per tide, ballast 10s each vessel [Daniel].

CHARLEMAGNE of Blakeney
178 tons (altered to 188 tons in 1881 with extra after deckhouse), 87.2 ft, 26.2 ft, 13.1 ft, date & place of build unknown, condemned by the Court of Admiralty 1861, brig, male face on gammon knee.
WSR 3/1863 (transferred from London) 19 Mar 1863 Benjamin Henry Nichols **64** merchant of Blakeney. 9 Apr 1863 B H Nicholls sold **5** to Douglas Baker ship insurance broker of Newcastle, and **5** to William Jarvis Boyce master mariner of Blakeney. 10 Apr 1863 B H Nichols sold **16** to John Howard butcher of Stiffkey, **10** to William Lown shipowner and butcher of Cley, **3** to Felix Ransome master mariner of Blakeney and **3** to Susanna Boyce dressmaker of Blakeney (White's 1864 *Norfolk Directory* – draper and milliner which implies a shop and larger enterprise than just dressmaking). 20 Apr 1863 B H Nicholls sold Robert Schollar master mariner of Morston and 28 May 1863 **6** to William Isaac Bensley shipowner of Blakeney (ex master mariner see **CHOICE**). Sept 1874 J Howard sold **16** to William Lown and 9 Nov 1878 B H Nicholls mortgaged **5** to Gurney & Co bankers of Fakenham for £150 + 5% interest, and 15 Feb 1879 Gurney sold these **5** on to W Lown. 3 Apr 1879 R Schollar sold **11** and W L Schollar sold **3** to W Lown (not clear when and from whom he bought these – possibly Susanna Boyce). 23 Mar 1882 F Ransome sold **3** and W I Bensley sold **3** to William Parsons master mariner of Blakeney. Apr 1866 sailed from Newcastle for Cronstadt (with coal?) [Osler].
7 Mar 1883 sold for breaking up.
Another large brig which may not have traded to her home port.

CHARLOTTE of Blakeney
20 tons, 34 ft 10 in, 12 ft 9 in, 6 ft 1 in, built 1807 at Wells, sloop, running bowsprit.
WSR 7/1843 & 2/1844 17 Apr 1843 James Jarvis **32** fisherman & skipper and John Loads fisherman both of Blakeney. 15 Dec 1843 J Loads sold **32** to J Jarvis.
1873 broken up.

CHARLOTTE of Cley
18 tons, 36.8 ft, 10.6 ft, 5.8 ft, built at 1823 Wells, sloop, running bowsprit.
WSR 4/1840 (previous Cley 1825), 5/1843, 3/1844, 15/1850 & 6/1854. 16 Mar 1840 Thomas Johnson **64** gentleman & master of Cley. 25 Mar 1843 re-registered tonnage changed to 13 tons same owner. 23 Jan 1844 rig now a smack William Dye the younger **64**. 26 July 1849 W Dye sells **16** each to James Lang Bale fisherman, Richard Pentney ship carpenter, John Billiny (?) coal merchant and George Balmin ship carpenter all of Blakeney. 12 July 1850 all sold **64** to John Sands farmer of Gunthorpe. 27 May 1854 J Sands sold **64** to Wm Loads senior & junior fishermen of Blakeney. 2 June 1854 W Loads junior sole owner.
1873 broken up.
Thomas Johnson's status as a gentleman suggests this vessel may have been a yacht which became a fishing vessel. Although a coal merchant was a shareholder, she is too small to be a cargo ship.

CHARLOTTE of Wells
93 tons, 66.6 ft, 17.3 ft, 10.2 ft, built at Wells by Thomas Henry Tyrrell, 7 Nov 1850, schooner, woman figurehead.
Master: Henry Ellis 1850.
WSR 17/1850 William Nettleton Gardner **48** gentleman (1851 Census farmer of 200 acres employing 4 men and 2 boys), and Robert Cubitt **16** merchant both of Wells. 1876 lost at sea.
William Gardner was a leading figure in the Independent Chapel, Wells, and a shareholder in the Wells & Fakenham Railway [*Norfolk News* 1851-57].

CHILDREN'S ADVENTURE of Wells
24 tons, 47.8 ft, 14.9 ft, 6.5 ft, built 1838 at Lowestoft, lugger (3 masts), changed to smack 1871, clench build.
WSR 2/1871 Joseph Dix **64** horticultural builder of Chelsea. 17 Apr 1872 J Dix sold **64** to Thomas William Hayhow shipwright of Wells.
30 Sept 1896 T W Hayhow sold 64 to John Doughty fisherman of Boston, registry transferred to Boston.
An intriguing first owner. Was she bought as a yacht and then her owner quickly lost interest and sold her?

CHOICE of Blakeney
99 tons, 62.9 ft, 18.1 ft, 11.2 ft built at Montrose, Scotland 1843, schooner, female bust. Master: Edward Lewis 1850.
WSR1/1850 (transferred from Arbroath) & 5/1860 William Isaac Bensley **32** and Isaac Mann **32** both master mariners of Blakeney. 1860 (transactions book) W I Bensley sold **32** to I Mann. 15 Jan 1873 I Mann sold **64** to Richard Horton shipowner of Grimsby and 15 Sept 1873 R Horton sold **64** to John Gresswell master mariner who sold her on on 26 Sept 1873 to John Gresswell master mariner of Hull.
20 Feb 1883 hulked registry at Wells closed.
Parliamentary Commission of Unseaworthy Ships 1873 no. 144 Feb 21 1874 '... *All low timbers aft rotten, several amidships and forward also, decks worn, stanchions rotten, treenails decayed, forecastle not properly drained, lit or ventilated. One boat 16 ft 12 in, 5 ft 8 in, 2 ft 3 in without buoyancy, lying at Hull, no master*'.

COCK-A-DOODLE-DOO of Wells or Blakeney
22 tons, smack, Official No. 86451, 4 crew, King's Lynn registered 6/1882.

COKE of Wells
42 tons, 53 ft, 13.5 ft, 6.9 ft, built at Louth, Lincs, 1827, sloop, topping up bowsprit, round stern, clench build.
Master: John Smith 1837, Christopher Kitwood 1865.
WSR 5/1827, 2/1837, 2/1846 & 6/1865. 15 Mar 1837 John Smith **21** mariner of Wells, Susan Crofts **22** widow of Wells with mortgage of £900 + interest to William Sherringham gentleman [White's 1844 *Norfolk Directory* maltster[, Fakenham and John Bakewell **21** victualler of Wakefield. 18 Jan 1846 W Sherringham 'by virtue of power of sale in the aforesaid indenture' sold **22** shares to Rev John Drake Crofts [curate at St Mary's] Little Walsingham for £150. 18 Feb 1846 re-registered in the names of Smith, Crofts [listed as merchant!]. 25 Aug 1853 Martin Browne solicitor and Jane Susanna Crofts spinster both of Little Walsingham and executors to the late Rev J D Drake sold **22** to William Cook master mariner of Wells. 18 Aug 1862 J Smith had acquired the other **42** shares and mortgaged them to John Savory merchant of Wells on £100+ 5% interest. 20 Oct 1863 Sarah Savory and John Savory junior merchant of Burnham inherit mortgaged **42** shares from late John Savory senior. Mortgage discharged 4 Oct 1867 and same day new mortgage to Robert Leamon shipowner [White's *Norfolk Dirctory* 1864 tanner] of Whitwell on £80 + 5% interest.
7 Sept. 1865 all **64** shares held by John Smith, shipowner of Wells, and last mortgage discharged 15 Jan 1875 and vessel sold to Benjamin Black and William Waddingham master mariner both of Barton-on-Humber. 22 Jan 1878 converted into lighter.
This was a billy boy possibly named after the Coke family of Holkham Hall, the local landowners of Wells and district. Along with Rev Beckwith of Wiveton, the Rev Crofts is another example of a clerk in holy orders holding shares in ships. The latter may have been related to George Crofts maltster and shipowner of Wells. Back in 1834, the Manor Court at Wells had taken out a commission in bankruptcy against Rev J D Crofts shipowner, dealer and chapman. At that time he had shares in the **ALBION** of 1814. One wonders what his bishop made of this. In 1845 the **COKE** made arrived from the 'Yorkshire rivers' 5 April, sailed on 12 for Hull, returned via King's Lynn on 19 April. On 7 June she arrived with coal from Goole, sailed on 2 August for 'the Yorkshire rivers' with wheat, sailed on 27 September in ballast from Goole, arrived on 4 October from Newcastle with coal, and on 15 November with coal from Goole, sailing on 29 for Goole with grain and arriving from Goole with coal on 27 Dec. This is an incomplete list but it gives a good idea of the voyage pattern of a small Wells coaster.

COMET of Blakeney
214 tons, 82.8 ft, 24 ft, 15.2 ft, built 1833 at Sunderland, Official No. 25336, snow, female bust (removed 1859).

Master: William White 1839.
WSR 10/1839 (transferred from Sunderland) & 1/1857. 11 Oct 1839 Robert John Brereton and Randle Brereton **32** each merchants of Blakeney. 4 Feb 1857 re-registered with Randle Brereton as sole shareholder.
6 Feb 1860 mortgaged to Harvey & Co bankers of Norwich.
21 Jan 1863 Harvey sold to Edwin Spence Roberts who on the same day sold to William Baxter of Robin Hood's bay, re-registered at Whitby.
The Breretons were maltsters and shipowners who owned ten vessels outright between 1840 and 1862 – five coasters and five deep sea ships.

COMMERCE of Cromer
63 tons, 59.8 ft, 16 ft, 8.3 ft, built 1800 at Wells, schooner. Master: 1840 William Rigden (see **ALBION** and **COMMERCE**).
Cley Reg 22/1836, WSR 5/1840 Henry Sandford **64** (coal) merchant of Cromer.
Re-registered at Stockton 26 Nov 1845.

COMMERCE (II) of Cromer
65 tons, 61.4 ft 16 ft, 8.9 ft, built 1846 by William Maston of Stockton-on-Tees, Official No. 6704, schooner
Master: William Rigden 1846.
WSR 4/1846 Henry Sandford **32** (coal) merchant and William Rigden **32** master mariner both of Cromer.
12 Jan 1858 sold and re-registered at Lowestoft. According to Clayton (1865) William Rigden remained as master. An older **COMMERCE** seems to have been taken in part exchange for this new ship. There is a photograph of the later **COMMERCE** on the beach at Cromer. She made 13 voyages between Cromer and Middlesborough between 7 Apr and 4 Dec 1861 [Malster, 1995: 5]
She was lost off the North Norfok coast13 Aug 1876.

CONCORD of Wells
55 tons, 60.4 ft, 16.9 ft, 8.2 ft, built 1839 by Thomas Cliffe at Knottingley, ketch, round stern, carvel & clench build.
Master: probably J Bramford 1861.
WSR 1/1861 Joseph Haycock junior **32** shipowner [coal & corn merchant –White's 1864 *Norfolk Directory*] and Joseph Bramford **16** master mariner and Susan Crawford **16** widow (of John Crawford, fisherman – 1851 Census) all of Wells. 1 Apr 1863 Susan Crawford married John Powditch shipowner [shipwright according to White's 1864 *Norfolk Directory*] of Wells who took over her shares.
23 November 1880 lost near Gainsborough (on the Trent). Knottingley on the River Aire was a hub for other waterways and a centre for building billy-boys [Gosney & Bowyer]. Notice how Susan Crawford was able to take over her shares on her marriage because this was before the Women's Property Act of 1870. See **CAROLINE** for further details of Joseph Haycock.

CONFIDENCE of Sheringham
27 tons, 42.4 ft, 13 ft, 6.8 ft, built 1841 at Sheringham, lugger (3 masts) round stern, running bowsprit, clench build.
Master: Robert Little 1841.
17 Apr 1841 Robert Sunman junior **16** boatbuilder [White's 1844 *Norfolk Directory* also wheelwright], John Brown **16** shoemaker of Gresham and John Denton **32** farmer of Bodham. 12 July 1842 R Sunman **16** to Charles Temple merchant of Blakeney as security for mortgage (sum not stated). 18 Aug 1843 C Temple sold **16** to Percival Arthur Upcher gentleman of Sheringham.
7 Aug 1859 re-registered at Gt Yarmouth.
The Upchers purchased an estate in Sheringham in 1812 and took an interest in the welfare of the local fishermen and their families. In 1836, the Hon Mrs Charlotte Upcher provided them with their own lifeboat, the **AUGUSTA,** built by Robert Sunman [Malster, 1974, p199].

CONSTANCE of Wells or Blakeney
20 ton smack, Official No. 69562. Registered at King's Lynn from Wisbech 2/1882

COSTA RICA of Blakeney (ex **AUDAX** of Guernsey & condemned by the Court of Admiralty 1873)
291 tons, 110.6 ft, 25.17 ft, 15.4 ft, built 1850 at unknown foreign port , barque (brig after 29 July 1877), female figurehead. Master: Henry Pinchen 1873.
WSR 1/1873 12 July 1873 William Isaac Bensley **64** shipowner of Blakeney. 15 July 1873 W I Bensley sold **8** shares to each to Robert Cubitt Wells merchant, Robert Oldham Wells master mariner all of Blakeney, and **8** to Henry Gifford Buck gentleman of Wiveton, Henry Pinchen master mariner of Cley, William Lown shipowner & butcher of Cley and to William Jarvis Boyce master mariner of S Shields; **4** to James Parker master mariner of Blakeney and William Nichols gentleman of Blakeney. 9 Dec 1874 R C Wells died and **4** shares went to his widow Harriett and Augustus Hill farmer of Blakeney.
27 Jan 1882 sold to Swedish owners.
Bensley retained only **8** shares and was clearly managing owner. He had had shares in 6 ships between 1850 and 1882 including **2** in the steam tug **WARRIOR** of 1871. Other landsmen – Cubitt and Lown were also experienced investors. Given her tonnage, it is unlikely that the **COSTA RICA** ever visited her home port.

COUNTESS OF LEICESTER of Wells
153 tons, 78.3 ft, 19.4 ft, 12.7 ft, built by Thomas Henry Tyrrell 20 Apr 1847, brig, female figurehead.
Master: John Sturley 1847.
WSR 11/1847 Henry Tyrrell **16** merchant [White's 1854 *Norfolk Directory* grocer & draper], George Wiseman **16** farmer and James Hull **16** merchant both of Burnham Overy, Tomas Thirtle Mack **8** merchant of Burnham Thorpe, William Mack **8** farmer of Burnham Norton and

The HELEN of Liverpool is similar in size and date to Joseph Haycock's full-rigged ship AGAMEMNON registered at Wells 1863-1872. (National Museums Liverpool)

John Groom **8** farmer of Walsingham. Further transactions 9 May 1857.
Sold c. 1864 to Jersey owners.
She was one of the finest ships built at Wells and was named after the Earl of Leicester's wife. This was possibly a piece of flattery as the Coke's of Holkham Hall were the chief landowners in the district and Tyrrell rented his shipyard from them. This ship was intended for deep-sea trade. For example between April and August 1850, she made a round voyage from London to Leghorn [Lloyd's List]. Henry Tyrrell was the shipbuilder's father and he took shares in 3 other ships built by his son. He may have had a shop in Blakeney as well and was involved in local administration including the Improvement Commissioners, the Harbour Commissioners and the Select Vestry. His second son Joseph John is believed to have made the diorama of the shipyard with the **COUNTESS OF LEICESTER** ready to be launched and John Sturley had a painting of her under sail off the Italian coast.

COUNTESS OF ZETLAND of Cley
184 tons, 87.1 ft, 22.7 ft, 14.2 ft, built 1845 at Grangemouth, Scotland, rig blank in register - probably a brig.
WSR 8/1858 17 Sept 1858 transferred from Leith, William T G Howes **64** shipowner [White's *Norfolk Directory* 1864 master mariner] of Cley. Same day W Howes sold **16** to Stephen Ampleford innkeeper of Cley [Craven's 1856 *Norfolk Directory* beer retailer & brewer], **8** to Clarke Painter yeoman, **24** to Howard Painter shipowner (probably painter & glazier) all of Cley. 19 June 1862 S Ampleford died and his executor Robin Cooke miller of Glandford sold his **16** shares to C Painter. 18 Oct 1862 H Painter died, his **24** shares were sold by his executors (Clarke Painter& Richard Newton schoolmaster of Blakeney) to W Howes.
1875 C Painter registered as managing owner. Fate unknown.

COURIER (ex- **COURIER DE ABBEVILLE**) of Blakeney
58 tons, 61.36 ft, 19.85 ft, 8.43 ft, Date and place of build unknown, schooner. Master: James Dew 1857.
WSR 6/1857 9 May 1857 Robert Cubitt Wells **64** merchant of Blakeney. 21 June 1857 R C Wells sold **21** to John Starling merchant & shipowner of Blakeney.
18 Jan 1861 lost, went ashore off Blakeney harbour.
Wells was a maltster and Starling was a corn miller [Craven's Norfolk Directory 1856] as well as a major shareholder in ships with shares in 9 vessels between 1843 & 1864.

CREST OF THE WAVE of Wells
153 tons, 81.7 ft, 19.2 ft, 11.5 ft, built 1854 by J S Southgate at Wells brig or snow.
WSR 3/1854 J S Southgate **64** shipbuilder & merchant of Wells.
3 Dec 1882 wrecked in the River Tees.
Joseph Southgate (1801 1877) was the leading businessman in Wells. He had multiple interests including corn, coal, porter and wine, ran a regular fortnightly service to London, and owned sixteen ships in total plus a share in the steam tug **ECONOMY**. He was one of the local directors of the Wells & Fakenham Railway which opened in 1857 and cost him much of his capital. This vessel was not re-registered after his death but was probably managed by his son Francis Southgate – the Wells postmaster. 1861 sailed from Newcastle to Morlaix, France (with coal?) [Osler].

CRISIS of Wells?
14 tons, yacht, Official No. 55316, King's Lynn registry 3/1900.

CYNTHIA of Sheringham
29 tons, 50.3 ft, 13.6 ft, 6.5 ft, built 1849 at Gt Yarmouth, Official No. 6761, lugger (3 masts), running bowsprit, round stern, clench build.
WSR 1/1852 9 Mar 1852 Richard Cox **64** fisherman and skipper of Sheringham.
Same date R Cox mortgaged **64** to Thomas Hudson victualler of Gt Yarmouth for £150+5% interest. 1869 transferred to Gt Yarmouth.

DAWN OF THE DAY of Wells or Blakeney
20 ton fishing smack, 4 crew, Official No. 29335, transferred from Gt Yarmouth 22/1861 and registered King's Lynn 3/1887.

DEFIANCE of Blakeney
38 tons, 55.8 ft, 16.5 ft, 10 ft, built 1832 at Sunderland, Official No. 3537, schooner, female bust. Master: William Mitchell.
SR 7/1854 & 6/1859 3 July 1854 (transferred from Inverness) John Starling **16** merchant [also miller and farmer in White's 1844 *Norfolk Directory*], William Starling **16** mariner, William Mitchell **16** mariner all of Blakeney and John Sayers **16** gentleman (also farmer) of Field Dalling. 9 May 1859 re-registered with W Mitchell as sole owner.
15 May 1863 sold to the Conservators (of Blakeney harbour) as derelict.

DEFIANCE of Cley
184 tons, built 1837 at Wells, brig. Master: William Ramm 1797-1838.
Probably registered at Cley, main shareholders the Musketts of Holt.
Norfolk Chronicle 20 Aug 1837 **DEFIANCE** on passage to Alexandria with coal, then to Odessa, 23 Dec 1837 at Odessa, 10 Feb 1838 wrecked at Kili 17 miles off the Bosphorus with a cargo of wool and tallow for Liverpool. Ramm and all hands lost except the cabin boy and the cook. Ramm left a wife and 6 children and a county-wide subscription raised £140 3s. [Dobson, 2010: 41-5]

DESPATCH of Wells
55 tons, 52.8 ft, 16.8 ft, 8.3 ft, built 1841 by J Parker at Wells, sloop, running bowsprit.
Master: Thomas Bunn 1841, John Coe 3 July 1849.
SR 9/1841, 14/1852 and 2/1860 9 Aug 1841 Thomas Dixon Sandling **64** coal merchant of Wells. 17 Feb 1847 T D Sandling mortgaged **64** to Edward Sheringham senior & junior farmers of Sculthorpe as security.
7 Sept the Sheringhams sell **64** to Joshua Gales merchant of Wells. 8 Aug 1860 J Gales sold **64** to Thomas Lord coal merchant of Wells (re-rigged as ketch). 9 June 1879 T Lord **32** each to George Proudfoot and Joseph Ransom master mariners of Wells. 16 Apr 1883 G Proudfoot sold **32** to Richard Francis Proudfoot butcher of Wells. 7 Oct 1884 J Ransom sold **32** to R F Proudfoot. 22 Jan 1886 R F proudfoot sold **64** to Frank Rust Lloyd manager of King's Lynn. 7 Mar 1887 F R Lloyd sells to owners outside Norfolk though Wells registration retained.
13 Sept 1893 lost off May Island.
1846 advert in *Norwich Mercury* announced the **DESPATCH** was replacing the wrecked **TRIAL** on the Wells-Hull packet service.

DIANA of Blakeney
201 tons, 103.3 ft, 21.6 ft, 12.8 ft, built 1853 at Murray harbour, Prince Edward Island, Canada, snow.
SR 14/1853 David Thomas **8** her master of Blakeney and seven other Newcastle shareholders.
18 Feb 1858 transferred to Newcastle. Prince Edward island was a prolific shipbuilding centre in mid-19th century and as its ships were cheaper than British ones, many were sold to British owners. See **ELECTRYON**.

DOVE of Blakeney & Cley
12 tons, 28.4 ft, 10.4 ft, 5.1 ft, built 1815 at Grimsby, sloop, running bowsprit. Master: Frederick Warnes.
SR 2/1843 & 6/1849 Thomas William Temple **32** merchant of Blakeney and Frederick Warnes **32** fisherman of Cley. 10 May 1849 T W Temple & F Warnes sold **32** to John Parker (fisherman?) of Stiffkey. 19 May 1849 John Baker shepherd of Stiffkey acquired all **64** shares.
7 Nov 1855 registry cancelled, broken up

DUKE OF WELLINGTON of Cley
91 tons, 64.4 ft, 17.3 ft, 10.6 ft, built 1840 at Hull by John Wright & Sons, schooner, male bust. Master: Robert Plattin 1840, Robert Moore 1843, possibly Robert Mann later [Mellor 1992: 31 and Mann family still have her portrait].
SR 13/1840 15 June 1840 Margaret Moore **24** merchant of Holt (later Cley), Thomas Beckwith **24** curate at Wiveton and resident of Holt, Clarke Painter shipowner [White's 1844 *Norfolk Directory* plumber & glazier of Cley and Holt], Robert Plattin **8** shipowner (and master) of Cley. 24 Oct 1843 Robert Plattin sold **8** to M Moore who sold them the next day to Robert Moore master mariner of Cley.
Oct 1845 wrecked in London.

EAGLE of Blakeney & Clay
14 tons, 32 ft 3 in, 10 ft 3 in, 4 ft 2 in, built 1818 at Cromer, sloop, runnning bowsprit, round stern. Master: James Jary.
SR 6/1840 (previously Cley 2/1830) 18 Aug 1840 Merrell Baines **64** fisherman of Blakeney.
8 Feb 1884 registry closed at request of owner as under 115 tons.

EAGLE of Wells or Blakeney
81 tons, schooner? 3 crew, Official No. 28714, wrecked 1900. King's Lynn registry 3/1896

ECHO of Wells
55 tons, dimensions? 55.4 ft, 16 ft, 6.1 ft, built Wakefield 1827 sloop, round stern, clench.
SR 12/1855 (Wells) James Allen **64** mariner of Burnham and master of the **ECHO**. 11 Nov 1856 dismasted off Brancaster, salvaged for further trading.
Re-registered at 14/1871 at Hull and transferred to Kings Lynn 5/1882 and wrecked again in 1883.
This was one of a number of upstream billy-boys acquired by N Norfolk shipowners. They regularly delivered grain and malt to Wakefield.

ECLIPSE of Wells
70 tons, 55 ft 7 in, 17 ft, 7 ft 2 in, built 1820 at Stockton-on-Tees, schooner, removing bowsprit.
Master: Thomas Powditch 1832, J Smith 1834.
SR 17/1832, 61833 & 6/1835 George Crofts **64** merchant of Wells. 22 Sept 1832 G Crofts mortgaged **32** to Joseph Springall Southgate shipowner and **32** to John Hammond Parker shipbuilder. 12 June 1833 mortgages discharged. 14 June 1833 George Croft acquired all **64** shares and mortgaged them to John Savory miller of Burnham Overy. 29 Mar 1834 G Crofts took out a 2nd mortgage with John Savory for £150 + interest. 3 July 1835 John Savory and George Crofts sold **64** (including mortgage) to J Savory to J S Southgate.
30 Jan 1836 wrecked.

ECONOMY of Wells
18 tons, 62 ft, 13.8 ft, 7.6 ft, built 1838 at N Shields, paddle sloop. Master: M R Parker.
SR 1/1840, 8/1848 & 5/1853 George Cross merchant, Michael Robinson Parker shipowner (and Lloyd's agent), Joseph Springall Southgate spirit merchant, William Elgar grocer, James Chapman merchant all of Wells and joint shareholders being five of the Commissioners for Improving the Harbour and Quay at Wells. 26 May 1848 all **64** shares sold to William Nettleton Gardner merchant (and farmer) of Wells. 21 Apr 1853 W N Gardner sold **32** to James Chapman aforesaid and **32** to James Byron Burton Sherston chemist & druggist of Wells. 17 April 1854 J B B Sherston sold **32** to James Chapman.
1870 registry closed, broken up.
This was the first steam tug at Wells and must have made a huge difference to access and the safety of the port. Like many paddle tugs she was built on the Tyne and would have been fitted with 2 side lever engines which could be worked independently to provide great manoeuvrability.

EDEN of Wells
76 tons, 60.6 ft, 16.5 ft, 9 ft, built 1838 by J H Parker at Wells, schooner, round stern. Master: James Powditch.
SR 6/1838 16 June 1838 Thomas Powditch **32** mariner of Wells and William Newman Frost **32** sailmaker of Wapping , Middlesex.
16 Oct 1847 vessel lost.
Frost had family links to Wells and may have originated from the town. He also invested in the new **NORFOLK TAR** in 1848 and the 3-master barque **GUADALETE** 334 tons & the biggest ship ever built at Wells.

EDWARD of King's Lynn
36 tons, 46.6 ft, 13.3 ft, 6.1 ft, built 1844 at Morston by John Raven Richardson, sloop, round stern. Master: John Hill
SR 10/1844 17 Aug 1844 William Richardson **32** of King's Lynn gentleman and John Raven Richardson **32** shipbuilder of Morston.
14 Aug 1845 J R Richardson sold **30** to W Richardson and 21 Sept re-registered at Cley.

EDWARD COKE of Wells
88 tons, 64.5 ft, 17 ft, 9 ft, built 1847 by John Lubbock. Master: John Lubbock.
SR 16/1847 25 Aug 1847 John Lubbock **64** shipbuilder of Wells. 3 Sept 1847 J Lubbock mortgaged **64** to Gurneys, bankers of Fakenham.
30 Aug 1848 L Lubbock sold **64** to Wisbech owners.
Lubbock probably built the **EDWARD COKE** as a speculation to keep his shipwrights in work. She was presumably named after a member of the Coke family of Holkham Hall – possibly the Earl's oldest brother of that name.

ELEANOR of Blakeney
78 tons, 67.3 ft, 5.9 ft, 8.4 ft, built 1847 at Hull, schooner, woman bust.
SR 4/1854 10 May 1854 John Starling merchant, miller etc **22** and Butcher Starling master mariner (and master) **21** and John Sayer **21** gentleman [White's 1844 *Norfolk Directory*] of Field Dalling. Field Dalling is a village 5 miles West of Holt and John Sayers was lord of the manor, hence the title gentleman.
21 July 1860 transferred to Maldon Register.
1870s owned by Robert Juniper malster, merchant and landlord of the *Ship Inn*, Mundesley [Malster, 1995, 6].

ELECTRYON of Cley
190 tons, 106.5 ft, 23.7 ft, 12.65 ft, built 1862 by McDougall at Grand River, Prince Edward Island, Canada brigantine, billet head.
SR 1/1863 10 Feb 1863 Samuel Cambridge Owen and John McDougall sold to Robert Henry Cooper **64** shipowner of Wiveton. 10 Sept 1879 R H Cooper sold **64** to John Knott, shipowner of Newcastle.
She was then sold to various other owners outside North Norfolk and transferred to the South Shields register on 9 Oct 1889.
Prince Edward Island was a prolific shipbuilding centre in mid 19th century; its products were cheaper than the British equivalent and were sold in substantial numbers to British owners. She would not have traded to Cley. Lloyds register for 1869 for example has her on a passage from Liverpool to the Black Sea. See **DIANA** as another example.

ELLEN of Burnham Overy
48 tons, 54.5 ft, 13.7 ft, 6.4 ft, built 1824 on River Hull, sloop, topping up bowsprit.
Master: William Parker 1837, William Durrant 2 Nov 1841, William Parker 30 Sept 1843.
SR 5/1837 (transferred from London 365/1835) 15 Nov 1837 William Parker **64** mariner of Burnham Overy.

ELLEN of Wells
91 tons, 62.6 ft 19.9 ft, 9.3 ft, built 1845 at Wells by Thomas Barber, schooner.
Master: Thomas Hayhow 1845, Robert Mussett 5 Aug 1850.
SR 1/1845 28 Jan 1845 Joseph Springall Southgate **64** merchant of Wells and same day mortgaged **64** to Robert Leamon of Whitwell gentleman [White's *Directory* 1844 tanner]. 2 Dec 1848 mortgage discharged. 31 Mar 1851 64 mortgaged to Gurney, Birkdale & Co bakers, Fakenham 'to secure payment on any floating balance' see **ELLEN** (II) and other Southgate ships.
7 Oct 1854 re-registered and probably sold after launch of **ELLEN** (II).

ELLEN (II) of Wells
116 tons, 75.1 ft, 17.6 ft, 9 ft, built 1854 by J S Southgate at Wells, schooner. Master: Robert Mussett 1854.
SR 13/1854 7 Oct 1854 Joseph Springall Southgate **64** merchant (shipbuilder) of Wells. 31 May 1857 J S Southgate mortgaged **64** to Gurney, Birkbeck & Co bankers of Fakenham 'on any floating balance'.
Lloyd's 1883 register had F Southgate as managing owner.
30 Sept 1883 wrecked at mouth of the Humber.
Joseph Southgate (1801-1877) was the leading entrepreneur in Wells with wide variety of business interests. He had shares in twenty-five ships between 1832 and 1860. He built six of them at his shipyard for his own use. He was involved in public administration and was a local director of the Wells & Fakenham Railway which cost much of his fortune.

ELIASAPH of Wells
21 tons, 56 ft, 12 ft 6.2 ft, built 1827 at Lowestoft, Official No. 21273, dandy smack, running bowsprit, clench. Master: John Lake.
SR 12/1854 29 Sept 1854 James Chapman **64** merchant of Wells
25 July 1858 lost off Dudgeon Lightship. Was she a yacht?

ELISA of Wells
15 tons, 36.2 ft, 11.1 ft, 5.7 ft, built at Wells 1814, sloop, running bowsprit. Master: William Crawford.
SR 1/1849 Henry Crawford **64** innkeeper of Wells.
1871 registry closed under 15 tons.
Henry Crawford was the landlord of the *Royal Standard* 1845-61 and was also an oyster merchant hence his ownership of the **ELISA** [Welland, 1912: 53]. Or was she used for smuggling?

ELIZA of Wells
21 tons, 36 ft, 12 ft 5 in, 5 ft 9 in, built 1814 at Wells, sloop, running bowsprit.
Master: Charles Belsham 1840, George Green 16 Aug 1841, James Morrison 20 Feb 1842, Robert Belsham 20 Apr 1844.
SR 17/1825, 3/1840, 4/1846 & 1/1849 26 June 1840 John Powditch **7** innkeeper (*Ship* 1836-42, 1857-65, *Red Lion* 1845-62 and foreman shipwright at Tyrrell's yard [Welland:2012: 75]), Robert Baker **3** baker, Isaac Newton **3** baker, John Brown **3** fisherman, Robert Sculfer senior **3** malster, John Leeder **3** shipwright, Robert Sculfer junior **3** shipwright, Robert Oliver Wells **3** shipwright , James Smith **3** mariner, Samuel Cable **3** mariner, Charles Belsham **3** mariner, Richard Belsham **3** carrier, Thomas Walker **3** husbandman, all of Wells. 14 Oct 1842 S Cable sold **3** to James Morrison mariner of Wells and **3** each purchased by James Cawley cordwainer and Robert Leeder blacksmith both of Little Walsingham and Edward Howard butcher of Stiffkey. 1 Dec 1845 all shareholders sold **64** to Henry Crofford (Crawford) innkeeper (*Royal Standard* 1845-61 of Wells [Welland , 2012: 74] These multiple shareholdings add up to fifty-seven and it looks as if the remaining seven were retained by the original owner who registered in 1825. His name is not stated. It is unclear why these working men invested in this fishing boat. The 3 shipwrights probably worked under Powditch and the 3 mariners may have made up the crew. The vessel was re-rigged as a smack in 1849 and continued to sail until at least 1871 when her registry was cancelled because she was under 15 tons. It is possible the **ELIZA** was bought to exploit the rich oyster beds that had been discovered off Wells in the 1820s or was this a smuggling venture?

ELIZA of Wells or Blakeney
17 ton fishing smack?, Official No. ?, King's Lynn registry 2/1899.

ELIZABETH of Cley
168 tons, 97 ft, 21.8 ft, 12.4 ft, built at Glasson Dock 1840, brig, female bust. Master: William Jary?
SR 9/1863 (transferred from Liverpool) 30 Dec 1863 William Allen **64** shipowner of Weybourne and same day sold **5** to William Jary master mariner of South Shields. 2 Jan 1864 W Allen sold **15** to William Lynes shipowner of Kelling, 11 Jan 1864 another **6** sold William Cooke gardener of Kelling and **3** to William Pigott master mariner of Weybourne. 20 Oct 1875 W Lynes sold **3** to J Holmes Bunwell carpenter of Holt.
This vessel was too big for her home port. William Allen owned a number of brigs in the Baltic trade.

ELLIS of Lowestoft
54 tons, built 1858 schooner. Master & owner: W B Payne.
One of the regular vessels delivering coal to Cromer before the arrival of the railway in 1877 [Clayton, 1865]. Between Feb and Dec 1871 she made 14 round trips between Cromer and W Hartlepool – 16 days to 4 weeks duration. Last trip from Cromer Mar 1887 but continued trading until 1920. She was nicknamed '**The Plumper**' because of her rather tubby lines [Malster, 1995, 6-7]

ELSIE of Wells or Blakeney
17 ton yacht, Official No. 43137, King's Lynn registry 3/1899.

EMILY of Burnham Overy
73 tons, 67.6 ft, 14.3 ft, 9 ft, built at S Shields 1854 schooner, female bust.
SR 6/1855 12 Feb 1855 Thomas Thirtle Mack **32** merchant, James Smith **16** master mariner and John Goddard Annis **16** master mariner (master) all of Burnham Overy.
11 Oct 1866 lost of East Bight Wells.
Thomas Mack was in partnership with Thomas Wiseman as corn & coal merchants and farmers. Both invested in ships: Mack in the **GEORGE & MARY** 1844, **HOPWELL** 1846 and 2 new ships built by Henry Tyrell **COUNTESS OF LEICESTER** and **MINSTREL** 1847. Wiseman in **FRIENDS** in 1841 with the other two Burnham Overy inhabitants.

EMMIE of Wells or Blakeney
17 ton steamer, possibly a tug, 3 crew, Official No. 80350.

ENCHANTRESS of Wells
116 tons, 64 ft, 18 ft, 11 ft, built 1852 by J S Southgate, Official No. 3426, schooner. Master: Benjamin Bower 1852.
SR 12/1852 26 Aug 1852 Joseph Springall Southgate **64** shipowner of Wells.
1869 lost.
Southgate was the leading entrepreneur at Wells see **ELLEN** etc.

ENDEAVOUR of Wells
40 tons, 54.8 ft, 12.8 ft, 5.7 ft, built ? sloop, topping up bowsprit, round stern, clench build.
Master: Thomas Harman 1836, John Alcock 10 Feb 1841.
SR 7/1832 & 21/1836 William Harman **64** innkeeper of Wells.
28 Oct 1842 sold to Thomas Teed, baker of Wisbech and re-registered there.

ENDEAVOUR of Brancaster
17 tons, 41.5 ft, 14.2 ft, 5.8 ft, built 1841 at Scarborough, yawl, round stern, clench.
SR 3/1857 (transferred from Boston) 4 Apr 1857 Thomas Hooks **32** master mariner and Thomas Rix 32 carrier both of Brancaster.
Dec 1860 lost on passage from Thornham to Newcastle.
Given her tonnage, one would have expected this vessel to be used for fishing but a passage to Newcastle suggests she was a cargo carrier.

ENDEAVOUR of Wells
68 tons, 60 ft, 16 ft, 8.3 ft, built 1843 by John Lubbock at Wells, schooner, top up bowsprit, round stern.
SR 3/1843 & 8/1855 30 Apr 1843 William Harman **64** shipowner and master. 19 Mar 1855 W Harman sold **32** each to John Curson merchant and Henry Crafer master mariner both of Wells.
19 Dec 1862 lost off Robin Hood's Bay on passage from Hartlepool to Wells with coal, crew of 5 saved.
John Curson gave evidence to the *Commission on Unseaworthy Ships* 1873.
William Harman (1781-1866) prospered through owning 4 ships, oyster dredging and fishing and also was landlord of the *Ship* in 1830 and the *Lugger* 1833-39 [Harman, 1995: 5-6].

ENDEAVOUR of Cley
201 tons, 89.7 ft, 23.7 ft, 14.35 ft, built 1850 at Sunderland, brig , female bust.
SR 1/1865 2 Jan 1865 William Taylor **64** merchant of Cley.
10 Dec 1871 lost.
Given her tonnage, she is unlikely to have called at her home port.

ENTERPRISE of Blakeney & Cley
107 tons, 67.5 ft, 18.7 ft, 11.2 ft, built 1842 by John Raven Richardson at Morston, rig probably schooner.
Master: Robert Wisker, John Cornhill 1847.
SR 4/1842 23 May 1842 Charles Temple **4** shipowner [White's 1844 *Norfolk Directory* merchant & maltster], Henry Bond **8** painter, Richard Newton **4** teacher, Thomas Hurn **8** shipowner [White's 1844 master mariner], Henry Ellis **4** shipowner [White's 1844 master mariner], William Bensley **4** master mariner, Eliza Wisker wife of Robert Wisker (master) and Hannah Nurse wife of William Ward Nurse master mariner **8**, all the above of Blakeney, John Francis Johnson **8** farmer of Salthouse, Robert Temple **8** farmer of Edgefield, Wigmore Howard **8** farmer of Stiffkey. 26 Feb 1846 Elizabeth Martha Johnson widow of J F Johnson inherited **8** shares and sold **4** and retained **4**. 22 Apr 1846 all shareholders sold **30** shares each to William James Bolding gentlman (farmer, maltster, miller and brewer) of Weybourne and William Monement cork manufacturer of King's Lynn. 21 June 1847 registry transferred to King's Lynn.
Here was a local enterprise: a large schooner built locally with local capital from a wide variety of shareholders. Morston Creek in Blakeney Harbour is to the west of Blakeney Quay and leads out to the Pit anchorage. John Richardson seems to have been an itinerant shipwright who only built the **ENTERPRISE** and the **EDWARD** before moving on. Very little was needed to set up a wooden shipbuilding yard beyond hand tools, a saw pit, a smithy and a steaming box – see the diorama of Tyrrell's yard at Wells (inside cover). Willam Bolding (1815-1899) was brother-in-law to William Monement cork merchant of Lynn and who married his sister Esther married in 1845 [Jefferson, 2003: 3].

ENVOY of Wells
147 tons, 83.9 ft, 20.6 ft, 11.8 ft, built 1846 at Tatagamouche, Nova Scotia, brig. Master: James Kerr.
SR 9/1847 18 May 1847 James Haycock the Younger **64** merchant of Wells. 24 Jan 1848 J Haycock mortgaged **64** to Major, Usborne & Co corn factors of London on £1000 + interest.
Registry closed 1867, supposed lost.
Is James Haycock the same as Joseph Haycock? It would seem so. He had shares in 7 vessels between 1847 and 1863. See for example **AGAMEMNON** or **CAROLINE** etc. This vessel was one of many ships built on Canada's eastern seaboard and exported to British owners in mid 19th century

EQUITY of Blakeney
116 tons, 70.3 ft, 21.1 ft, 11.4 ft, built 1802 at Scarborough, brigantine. Master: S Jordon 1834.
SR 14/1856 Randle Brereton **64** merchant of Blakeney. 6 Feb 1860 **64** mortgaged with several other vessels to Harvey & Co, bankers of Norwich. 25 Mar 1863 Harveys sell **64** to Edward Spence Roberts, shipowner, Jerusalem Coffee House, London.
18 Dec 1863 E S Roberts sold **64** to John Ward of Sunderland and re-registed at Sunderland.

EUPHEMIA of Blakeney
141 tons, 71.3 ft, 19.5 ft, 13.2 ft, built 1839 at Leith, brig, woman bust.
SR 3/1851 7 Apr 1851 Thomas Mitchell **32** shipowner Blakeney and William Mitchell master mariner (master) **32**. 9 Dec 1851 T Mitchell sold **11** to W Mitchell.
4 Oct 1852 lost on Ship Wash Sand.

EXPERIENCE
Owned by William Partridge Cubitt (1818-1884) of Bacton, foundered off Sunderland at unknown date, all crew lost.

FAITH of Brancaster
43 tons, 53.9 ft, 12.8 ft, 5.7 ft, built at Knottingley 1826, sloop, round stern, carvel & clench build.
Master: S Bastard 1834.
WSR 3/1849 5 Mar 1849 John Mussett **32** master mariner and master of Brancaster and Thomas Southeren mariner **32** of Titchwell '*who being at a greater distance than 20 miles cannot attend the Customs House*'. 8 May T Southeren sold **32** to Elizabeth Mussett widow.
1870 registry closed, disabled for sea.

FANNY of Cley
106 tons, 68 ft, 18 ft 11.1 ft, built 1825 at Ipswich, brig. Master: J Jary 1834, Thomas Hayhow.
WSR 12/1839 25 Oct 1839 Joseph Muskett **7** and Willaim Muskett **9** shipowners of Holt [White's Norfolk Directory 1844 grocers & drapers with a branch at Cley], William Thomas **8** shipowner of ?, Howard Ramm **8** shipowner (master mariner) of Cley, Ann Ellis **1** spinster of Cley, Daniel Newton **8** grocer, Samuel Smith **8** attorney, Lucy Barnes **8** widow all of Blakeney, Lucy Ann Smith **4** spinster of Bungay. 11 Aug 1842 both Musketts mortgaged **10** shares as part security on £1500 + interest to Parlett Starling Esq of Norwich. 4 May 1844 all shareholders sold up to the Musketts, 8 May 1844 they in turn discharged their mortgage.
The Musketts brought together a group of mainly non-maritime investors in five ships in the 1840s and they were the sort of ships to serve them in delivering groceries and draperies from London. They had maritime expertise with Howard Ramm (1786-1862) who had commanded his first ship back in 1819. Ramm had a wide range of commercial interests in Cley including property and a shop dealing in pottery. His father-in-law was Daniel Newton who was stepfather to his wife Elizabeth[Dobson: 2010. 35-38]. There were probably other family connections. It is likely that Samuel Smith and Lucy Ann Smith of Bungay were related.

FH of Wells or Blakeney
19 tons fishing smack, Official No. 91609, first registered at King's Lynn from Gt Yarmouth 18/1875 and re-registered KL 1/1887.

FLYING CHILDERS of Blakeney
84 ton paddle tug, clench build.
Transferred from Hull and registered at King's Lynn 1/1899. This is uncertain because most records show her to be stationed at Great Yarmouth. She was named after a famous early 18th century race horse

FOUR BROTHERS of Wells or Blakeney
18 tons,fishing smack, Official No. 67417.
Transferred from Gt Yarmouth. King's Lynn registry 1/1890

FRANK of Cromer
Schooner? Master and owner: William Jarvis.
Foundered off Isle of Wight with cargo of Caen stone. Master and crew rescued [Malster, 1995: 4].

FREDERICK & BETSY
50 tons, 55 ft, 13.5 ft, 7.2 ft, built 1825 at Louth, Lincs, schooner, topping up bowsprit, round stern, clench build.
Master: Thomas Hubbard 29 Apr1843, Christopher Kitwood 7 Nov 1843, Thomas Luke Harman 7 Nov 1845.
WSR 24/1836 26 Aug 1836 William Harman (1781-1866) **64** innkeeper (The *Ship* 1830-35 and the *Lugger* 1836-39 [Welland, 2012: 35 & 57]) also master 1836 –1843. 1 Jan 1846 W Harman sold **64** to Francis Loose plumber & glazier of King's Lynn and Thomas Luke Harman master mariner (and 3rd son of W Harman) of Wells.
William Harman was also a pilot, fisherman and bought property in Wells [Harman, 1995: 5-6]. Louth might seem an od place to

build even a small billy-boy. The Louth Navigation was a part canalization of the River Lud from the market town of Louth to Tetney Haven on the Humber and opened in 1767. Sea-going vessels were quite often built well inland in the early 19th century e.g Norwich or Ely [Paget-Tomlinson, 1978: 184].

FRIENDS of Wells
10 tons, 29.5 ft, 10.5 ft, 5.3 ft, built at King's Lynn 1824, smack, running bowsprit, clench build.
Master: William Crofford (Crawford)
WSR 10/1824, 8/1844 & 3/1853 5 Oct 1844 Henry Crofford (Crawford) master & victualler at the *Royal Standard*, Wells. 23 Mar 1853 H Crofford sold **64** to Henry Sutherland (or Southerland) fisherman of Brancaster.
26 Jan 1865 registry cancelled, broken up.

FRIENDS of Burnham Overy
36 tons, 44 ft, 14.4 ft, 7.5 ft, built 1841 by John Lubbock at Wells, sloop, running bowsprit.
Master: James Atkins 1841, John Howell 22 Jan 1849.
WSR 6/1841 & 8/1859 6 May 1841 Thomas Wiseman merchant [White's *Norfolk Directory* 1844 also farmer] **22**, James Hull merchant (corn, coal & coke), John Savory **21** miller all of Burnham Overy. 13 May 1847 J Hull's executors sold **21** to Thomas Thirtle Mack merchant at Burnham Overy & farmer at Burnham Thorpe. 21 June 1859 J Savory junior **43** (presumably having acquired Wiseman's shares). 27 May 1859 J Hall (or Hull junior) died and his executors sold **21** to J Savory junior.
5 Feb 1864 lost at Donna Nook, Lincs (the southern entrance point of the Humber).
This group of merchant farmers along with Savorys the millers all had interest in shipping their goods into Burnham Overy and Hull and Mack went on to take shares in a deep-sea vessel, the new **COUNTESS OF LEICESTER** of 1847.

FROLIC of Wells
11 tons, 34.7 ft?, 10,7 ft, 5.6 ft, built 1851 by James Morrison at Wells, 2 masts (schooner/ketch?) running bowsprit, clench build.
31 May 1851 James Morrison **21** fisherman and skipper of Wells.
John Gibbs **43** mariner of London. 4 Oct 1854 J Gibbs sold **43** to J Morrison.
It was unusual for such a small vessel to be schooner rigged. Perhaps she was a racing vessel. Gibbs 'master mariner' occupation might hide a wealthier position

FRUITERER of Wells
71 tons, 56.6 ft, 17.6 ft, 9.5 ft, schooner, lute stern, female bust.
WSR 8/1847 13 May 1847 Francis Sculfer **64** master mariner (and master) of Wells. 13 Feb 1849 F Sculfer sold **24** shares to Robert Sculfer maltser of Wells (possibly the innkeeper of the *Green Dragon* 1830-35 [Welland, 2012: 27].
4 Apr 1853 sold to Hull owners and re-registered there.
The name **FRUITERER** suggests that this schooner was designed for the fruit trade. This was a seasonal business (mainly in the Autumn) collecting cargoes Mediterranean fruits such as grapes, oranges and dried raison, currants etc. There was also a big trade in oranges from the Azores and pineapples from the West Indies. It required fast ships to deliver these perishable cargoes intact. London was the main centre of the trade but small fast ships from many provincial ports competed.

GELDESTONE of Wells
34.45 tons, 46.5 ft, 14.8 ft, 5.8 ft, built 1828 at Wakefield, sloop, round stern, carvel and clench build.
WSR 15/1856 (transferred from Gt Yarmouth) John Rix **64** master mariner of Wells and **64** shares mortgaged to Benjamin Powson, merchant of Gt Yarmouth to secure £150 + 5%.
30 Apr 1870 broken up.
The mortgage probably represented the purchase price of this billy-boy @ £4.35 per ton.

GEM of Wells
68 tons, 76.8 ft, 17.5 ft, 8.7 ft built 1856 by Henry Tyrrell, Wells, schooner.
WSR 10/1856, 25 Sept 1856 Robert Leeder **32** shipowner and innkeeper of the *Sun* 1839-1865 of Wells [Welland, 2012: 62] and John Howard Butcher **32** butcher of Stiffkey. 7 Nov 1867 executors of J Howard sold **32** to R Leeder and same day Leeder sold **32** to James Cook master mariner of Wells who took out a mortgage with Leeder for £200+4% interest. This was discharged on 27 Jan 1868? 1869 J Cook died and left **32** shares to Sarah his widow and 19 Dec 1877 Sarah Cook married Samuel Bell grocer & draper of Wells who took over her shares.
23 Apr 1889 lost in collision with **SS GREGORY** 6 miles off Folkestone.

GEM of Blakeney
39 tons, 63.8 ft, 14.5 ft, 7.5 ft, 20 HP built 1857 at N Shields paddle sloop, round stern, clench build.
WSR 4/1863, 19 Mar 1863 Charles Temple **44** merchant of Blakeney, James William Porritt **20** merchant of Cley. Same day Charles Temple sold **8** shares each to B H Nichols merchant, David Thomas and George Thompson master mariners all of Blakeney. 11 April 1863 G Thompson mortgaged **8** shares to William Temple, gentleman of Blakeney on £90 +5% interest ; this was discharged 30 May 1871. Same day executors of D Thomas transferred **8** shares to Mary Ann Thomas, his widow, and also the same day the tug was sold by all shareholders to William Brown steam tug owner of Monkwearmouth.
13 Nov 1872 transferred to Sunderland registry.
This was the first tug in Blakeney harbour arriving 23 years after the **ECONOMY** at Wells. She would have been used not only for bringing in vessels from the sea but also lighterage from the Pit anchorage and to Cley where the channel was becoming increasingly shallow.

This three masted lugger at Great Yarmouth in the 1820s was similar to the Sheringham three-masted luggers. The wheels in the background are part of the lifting mechanism of the bridge between Yarmouth and Southtown.

GEORGE of Wells
Schooner, built 1829 at Wells, owners R Parker [Lloyd's 1834]. Master: R Holmes.

GEORGE of Wells
Master: S Woods, owner S Greig [Lloyd's 1834].

GEORGE AND HANNAH of Wells
13 tons, 35 ft 11.9 ft, 5.2 ft, built 1837 at Wells by George Empson, smack, running bowsprit, clench build.
WSR 3/1837 George Empson **64** fisherman of Wells.
Oct 1868.
It was unusual but entirely possible for a fisherman to build his own boat. There is no record of Empson building anything else though he might have built small open boats which would not have been registered. While most fishing craft have been omitted this vessel is included because of its local construction and is typical of the small smacks that used the port.

GEORGE AND MARY of Burnham Overy
72 tons, 58.8 ft, 15.2 ft, 8.3 ft, built 1840 at Doncaster, schooner, round stern. Master: James Atkins.
WSR 4/1844, 13/1846 & 12/1856, 23 Feb 1844 Thomas Thirtle Mack **22** farmer of Burnham Thorpe, George Wiseman **21** farmer of Burnham Overy and William Mack **21** farmer of Burnham Sutton. 21 Dec 1846 all three shareholders sold to Thomas Powditch **22** shipowner, James Powditch **21** innkeeper of Wells (this could be John as Welland only lists a John), and John Savory **21** corn factor (and miller) of Burnham Overy. 18 Oct 1856 the Powditch and John Savory sold **64** to Thomas Lord, coal merchant of Wells.
21 Nov 1872 run down in Hull Roads.
The early sale by the three farmers suggests that they could not make the ship pay. But it did not stop Thomas Thirtle Mack later investing in other vessels.

GEORGE AND MARY of Wells or Blakeney
31 ton fishing smack, 4 crew, Official No. 18494.
Transferred from Gt Yarmouth to King's Lynn 2/1891

GEORGE AND WILLIAM of Burnham Overy
63 tons, 58.8 ft, 15.8 ft, 7.6 ft, built 1849 at Goole, schooner, top up bowsprit, round stern. Master: William Cringle 1854.
WSR 9/1854 14 July 1854 James Hull merchant **13**, Thomas Thirtle Mack **13** (merchant and farmer), James Smith **13** and William Cringle **13** master mariners all of Burnham Market, and Samuel Bullard **12** shipping agent of 39 Great Tower St, London.
8 Oct 1856 vessel sold to ?
This billy-boy schooner almost certainly served Hull and Mack's businesses at Burnham Overy. Samuel Bullard came from the

Burnhams and was a master mariner who went into partnership with Daniel King as shipowners and brokers in London. They ran small sailing ships to the Mediterranean and in 1858 set up a pioneer service to Natal. In 1859, they had the 253 ton barque **PRISCILLA** built at Wells by Henry Tyrrell for this service.

GEORGE HUGHES of Wells
234 tons, 101.8 ft, 25.7 ft, 14.3 ft, built 1853 at St Ann's, Cape Breton, Canada, 3 masted barque, 1 deck with round house, scroll figurehead.
WSR 3/1864 15 Aug 1864 Robert Leamon **64** merchant [White's 1864 *Norfolk Directory* tanner] of Whitwell Hall. 19 June 1871 R Leamon sold **64** to Thomas Moore master rigger of Sunderland, and William Robertson master mariner of Blyth.
27 Nov 1876 converted into hulk.
Evidence for the *Commission for Unseaworthy Ships* 13 Mar 1874 at Sunderland laden with coal and flints for Eggersund, Norway; discharged 40 tons of flint and now has a clear side (freeboard?) of 3 ft 9 in; poor caulking with local leak which caused her detetention. Two boats, one useless, the other not buoyancy, needs rowlocks and thwarts. Repaired and released.
This vessel was one of many ships built on the Eastern seaboard of Canada and exported to Great Britain at prices much lower than the British equivalent. What an affluent tanner doing owning a barque is unclear. His only other shipping interests were **21** shares in the 42 ton **OLIVE BRANCH** and **42** for a mortgage on the **COKE** in 1867. He may have been related to Robert Lemon or Leamon (it was spelt both ways) who took over Tyrrell's yard from 1863 to about 1869-70. The **GEORGE HUGHES** was probably not employed out of Wells. It is far more likely she was in the Baltic timber trade.

GIPSEY of Blakeney
92 tons, 64 ft, 19 ft, 10 ft, built 1853 at Jarrow, brig.
WSR 5/1856 Isaac Mann **16**, Samuel Daniels **16**, William Isaac Bensley **16** and Miles Lane **16**, all master mariners of Blakeney.
20 Dec 1863 lost.
Bensley, Daniels and Mann were experienced shipowners, and Bensley and Mann had already run the schooner **CHOICE** since 1850.

GLADIATOR of Wells or Blakeney
24 tons fishing smack, 4 crew, Official No. 56301.
Transferred from Gt Yarmouth to King's Lynn 9/1887

GLAVEN of Blakeney
19 tons, 43.4 ft, 13.1 ft, 4 ft, built 1841 by Thomas Claxton, Official No. 21261, 2 masted lugger, running bowsprit, round stern.
Master: Edward Baines 1841.
WSR 6/1841 William Cooke **26** shipowner of Glandford, Robin Cooke **26** shipowner of Thornage and John Baines **12** shipowner of Blakeney.
1874 registry cancelled converted to a lighter.
The Cookes owned watermills at Glandford and Thornage and were also shipowners and merchants. They commissioned their first ship the 85 tons schooner **HEBE** from J H Parker at Wells in 1839 and purchased another 4 up to 1849. The **GLAVEN** was a sailing barge for use around Blakeney Harbour. There is a photograph of two such barges at Cley around 1880 in *Archive* No. 2.

GLEANER of Wells
Master: H Watson [Lloyd's 1834]

GLEANER of Wells
71 tons, 58.6 ft, 16.5 ft, 8.2 ft, built 1844 by J S Southgate at Wells, schooner.
Master: James Sturley 1844, Edward Sturley 2 June 1849, James Sturley 21 June 1850 at Hartlepool, Thomas Newton 8 Oct 1853 at Newcastle.
WSR 7/1844 7 7/1857 3 May 1844 Joseph Springall Southgate **43** merchant, shipbuilder etc and James Sturley **21** master mariner both of Wells. 4 May 1844 J Sturley took out of a mortgage with J S Southgate and this was discharged 18 Jan 1849. 4 Feb 1854, vessel sold & re-registered at London. 1856 **64** shares purchased by Joseph Haycock junior merchant of Wells. 28 Dec 1866 J Haycock sold **64** to William Jecks timber merchant of Beccles.
9 Aug 1867 lost off Robin Hood's Bay.
Joseph Southgate was the leading shipowner and merchant at Wells. While under his ownership in 1845 according to the *Norfolk Chronicle* shipping reports she regularly delivered grain to the Humber ports and returned from Newcastle with coal.

GLEE of Wells or Blakeney
24 tons, fishing smack?, 4 crew, Official No. 45296.
Transferred from Colchester to King's Lynn 1/1888.

GLENMORISTON of Wells
66 tons, 59.5 ft, 16.2 ft, 9.1 ft, built 1820 at Invermoriston, Inverness, schooner.
WSR 9/1838 (transferred from Newcastle) Edward Lubbock **64** mariner (and master) of Wells. 16 Jan 1840 E Lubbock mortgaged **64** to Mary Hollis West spinster of Wells and this mortgage discharged 22 May 1841. 2 Sept 1840 took out a 2nd mortgage with John Palmer gentleman of Gt Yarmouth and this discharged on same day. 10 June 1841 E Lubbock took out another mortgage on **64** shares with John Scarborough gentleman of Tokenhouse Yard, London.
20 Aug 1841 E Lubbock sold **64** to William Frost ship chandler of Wapping, Middlesex.
A short-lived master mariner's venture financed by loans. Frost who was listed elsewhere as a sailmaker seems to had a

connection with Wells and in 1854 ordered Henry Tyrrell to build the biggest ship ever built in Wells – the 334 ton 3 masted barque **GUADALETE**.

GOOD INTENT of Wells
109 tons, 65.2 ft, 18.4 ft, 9.2 ft, built at Wells 1829, snow. Master: James Smith 1836, James Race 30 Mar 1838 at Goole, John Dunn 23 Feb 1839 at Wells, William Watson 4 Oct 1839 at Newcastle, Thomas Walker 3 Dec 1840 at Stockton, William Smith 27 July 1841 at Stockton, Thomas Walker 25 Sept 1841 at Wells.
WSR 10/1830 & 25/1836 29 Dec 1836 Susan Crofts **56** widow, John Wiseman mariner **8**. There were existing mortgage of of 26 July 1830 and 18 Dec 1834 to William Sherringham, gentleman of Fakenham. 7 Sept 1842 J Wiseman sold **8** shares to Charles George Crofts merchant of Liverpool. 11 Oct 1842 S Crofts and W Sherringham sold **56** to G C Crofts 'without incumbrances' and the same day G C Crofts re-mortgaged the ship to W Sherringham.
Probably transferred to Liverpool. It looks as if G C Crofts was the son Susanna and George Crofts (deceased) maltster, merchant and shipowner and that he had moved to Liverpool to seek his fortune. The changes of master show the **GOOD INTENT** was on the coal and grain run to the Humber and the North East.

GREAT GLORY of Sheringham
11 tons, 31.7 ft, 10.2 ft, 5 ft, built 1835 at Sheringham 2 masted lugger, running bowsprit, round stern, clench build.
Master James West 1838.
Clay 16/1838, WSR 5/1846 12 May 1846 Barcham Barcham **64** gentleman of Sheringham.
2 Feb 1849 sold to Robert Hain, fisherman of Gorleston and re-registered at Gt Yarmouth.
She is typical of the 30 or so 'Great Boats' which were 3 masted luggers mainly owned in Sheringham with smaller numbers at Runton, Cromer, Overstrand and North Repps. They followed the herring fishing from Yorkshire down the autumn fishery at Yarmouth and at other times of the year could go long-lining for cod and also catch crabs. They were lay up for the winter at Wells or Great Yarmouth. By the 1890s many were converting from lug to a loose-footed mainsail and abolishing the 3rd mast [Malster, *Ships Monthly* 4: 442].

GREAT UPCHER of Sheringham
23 tons, 43.4 ft, 13.5 ft, 6.2 ft, built 1841 at Scarborough, 2 masted lugger, running bowsprit, round stern, clench build. Master: Henry West 1841.
WSR 11/1841 & 10/1851 2 Aug 1841 Henry West junior **32** and William West **32** both fishermen of Sheringham. 1 May 1851 the Wests sell **64** shares to Joseph Nightingale & Benjamin Johnson fishermen of Sheringham. 22 July 1854 J Nightingale & B Johnson sold **64** shares to William & Robert Johnson both fishermen of Sheringham.
1886 broken up.
The name is presumably in honour of the Upcher family of Sheringham Hall who were concerned with the welfare of the local fishermen and provided them with a lifeboat in 1836.

GREEK SLAVE (ex **ARIETA**) of Wells
127 tons, 71 ft, 23 ft, 15.3 ft, foreign built at unknown, brigantine.
WSR 2/1863 12 Feb 1863 Joseph Springall Southgate **64** merchant of Wells. In 1875 J S Southgate sold **64** shares to William Watson master mariner of Wells who then mortgaged the vessel to Southgate for £300 (possibly the purchase price) and on J Southgate's death in 1877 the mortgage was transferred to Francis Southgate merchant of Wells.
F Southgate eventually sold her to Chambers & Page shipbuilders of Lowestoft in 1886.
By 1889, she had been abandoned on Breydon Water and was photographed by P Emerson for his book *Wild Life on a Tidal Water* published in 1889.

GREENWOOD of Wells
58 tons. Master: Smithen [Lloyd's 1834]

HALCYON of Blakeney
286 tons, 99.5 ft, 26.1 ft, 16.3 ft, built 1852 at Sunderland, snow, three quarter length female figurehead.
SR 7/1866 (transferred from Newcastle) 31 Apr 1866 Robert Watson **64** shipowner of Newcastle. 29 Apr R Watson sold **64** to Benjamin Nicholas shipowner [Craven's 1856 Norfolk Directory coal merchant, Westgate St]. 31 Apr 1866 B Nichols sold **8** each Douglas Cooper, shipbroker of Gateshead and Robert Watson as above. 9 July 1866 B Nichols sold **14** to William Jarvis Boyce master mariner of Blakeney and **5** to Susanna Boyce milliner of Blakeney. 18 July 1866 B Nicholls sold **8** and **7** to James Parker and Felix Ransome both master mariners of Blakeney. 11 Sept B Nichols sold **6** to Robert Schollar boatman of Morston. 26 Apr 1867? W J Boyce sold **3** to John Long miner of Bedlington, Northumberland. 8 Nov 1878 B Nichols mortgaged **8** for £200+5% interest to Gurney & Co, bankers of Fakenham and 30 Nov 1879 Gurneys foreclosed and sold **8** shares to Charles John Jary master mariner of Blakeney. 28 Aug 1879 Robert Schollar sold **6** C J Jary.
10 Sept 1879 R Watson sold **8** to John Ridley Watson shipbroker of Newcastle. 26 Sept 1879 J Parker died and left **8** shares to his widow Susanna (J Parker must have married Susanna Boyce and taken on her **8** shares) and 17 Sept 1881 she sold them on to J R Watson. 14 Sept 1881 J R Watson sold **8** to John Lee shipowner of Newcastle. 1 Nov 1883 D Cooper sold his **8** to J R Watson.
7 Oct 1886 all shareholders sold vessel to Danish owners.
There may be some missing transactions as Nichols ended up **3** shares by July 1866. Given the tonnage of the vessel and the Newcastle links, it is likely that she traded mainly out of the Tyne.

HANNAH of Cromer
12 tons, 32 ft, 10.7 ft, 4.8 ft built 1838 at Trimingham by Thomas Hull, Official No. 6798, 3 masted lugger, running bowsprit, round stern, clench build.
SR 5/1841 10 May 1841 William Copsey **32** and Henry Neckells **32** both fisherman of Cromer. 8 Mar 1859 registry cancelled as under 15 tons. This lugger was probably built on the beach at Trimingham. This was not unusual in the early 19th century as wooden shipbuilders required little equipment or buildings. Could Thomas Hull in fact be Thomas Hall who was a wheelwright, pumpmaker and landlord of the *Crown & Anchor* according to White's *Norfolk Directory* for 1844?

HANNAH of Burnham Overy
46 tons, 48.8 ft, 15.6 ft, 7.5 ft, built at 1834 at S Shields. Master: Henry Bush 1841, Thomas Hubbard 19 Sept 1844.
SR 4/1841 & 4/1849 7 Apr 1851 Henry Bush **64** shipowner of Burnham Overy [White's 1845 *Norfolk Directory* victualler at the *Jolly Sailors*, Burnham Overy]. 10 Mar 1849 Robert Thurston Loynes solicitor of Wells and executor to H Bush deceased sold **64** shares to Peter Cooper malster of Burnham Overy.
21 Nov 1855 transferred to King's Lynn registry

HANNAH of Cley
125 tons, 74.1 ft, 28.8 ft, 12.3 ft, built 12 Aug 1850 at Wells, snow, female bust.
SR 2/1858 3 Feb 1858 William Gibbs **32** merchant [White's *Norfolk Directory* 1864 innkeeper of the *Fishmongers' Arms*], William Henry Gibbs **8** merchant both of Cley, Thomas Lynes **8** gardener of Kelling, Richard Shore **8** innkeeper of Gt Yarmouth.
11 Apr 1863 transferred to Gt Yarmouth and according to Clayton's *Directory* 1865, she was re-rigged as a brigantine and owned by W H Gibbs of Cley.

HANNAH of Wells
139 tons, 71.4 ft, 18.7 ft, 12.3 ft, built 12 Aug 1850 by J S Southgate, Official No. 14206, snow, female figurehead.
Master: Thomas Hughes 1850, John Hendry 9 May 1854.
SR 16/1850 13 Aug 1850 Joseph Springall Southgate **64** shipowner and merchant of Wells. 9 Dec 1950 J S Southgate mortgaged **64** to Gurney, Birkbeck & Co, Fakenham.
Sold or wrecked sometime before 1865.
Joseph Southgate (1801-77) was the leading entrepreneur of Wells as a merchant, shipbuilder and shipowner.

HANNAH AND MARY of Wells or Blakeney
366 tons, 122.8 ft, 28.1 ft, 17.5 ft, 1868 by Barker at Sunderland, 3 masted barque.
Registered 65, 1868 at King's Lynn, owners at Wells or Blakeney.
Sold foreign 22 Nov 1890.

HAPPY HOME of ?
24 ton cutter SR King's Lynn 7/1882, Official No. 36452.

HAPPY RETURN of Cromer
9 tons, 32 ft, 9.6 ft, 4 ft, built 1814 at Trimingham, 2 masted lugger, running bowsprit, round stern, clench build.
SR 20/1840 Thomas Randall **64** fisherman of Cromer.
Oct 1851 broken up.
Like the **HANNAH** this lugger was built in an unusual place.

HAPPY RETURN of Sheringham
16 tons, 33 ft 2 in, 10 ft 9 in, 4 ft 7 in, built 1833 at Sheringham 3 masted luggers, running bowsprit, round stern, clench build.
Master: John Davies.
SR 15/1847 & 10/1848 Thomas Randall **64** fisherman of Sheringham.
4 May 1848 T Randall sold **64** to John Davies senior and junior fishermen of Cromer.
1870 broken up.

HAPPY RETURN of Brancaster
17 tons, 37.4 ft, 13.2 ft, 4.8 ft, built 1835 at Scarborough, 2 masted lugger, round stern, clench build.
WS 3/1867 (transferred from King's Lynn) 31 Apr 1867 George Southerland **64** master mariner. 13 Apr 1890 G Southerland died and **64** left to George Southerland farmer of Brancaster Staithe. 27 Feb 1891 G Southerland (2) sold **64** to Thomas Loose fisherman of Brancaster Staithe.
4 Apr 1893 unseaworthy, registry cancelled.

HARRIET AND ANN of Blakeney
30 tons? 38 ft 10 in, built 1823 at Blakeney, sloop, running bowsprit. Master: William Lincoln 1842.
WS 1/1842 Charlotte Lincoln **64** widow.
27 Oct 1855 registry cancelled, broken up.

HEBE of Blakeney
44 tons, 52.7 ft, 15.1 ft, 8.4 ft, date of build unknown, formerly **BARTHOLOMEW** taken as a prize by **HMS RANGER** (possibly frigate of 1818) a smuggler probably, sloop, running bowsprit.
WS 11/1839 William & Robin Cooke **32** each millers of Glandford and Thornage.
Probably broken up in 1849.

HEBE of Blakeney
75 tons, 64 ft, 19 ft, 6 ft, built at 1839 Wells, schooner.
SR 6/1844, 10/1853 & 3/1856 27 Feb 1856 Henry Nicholls **16**, master mariner, Ben Nicholls **16** master mariner and James Parker **16** master mariner all of Blakeney and John Cooke **16** shipowner. Sold 1853 to Robin & William Cooke millers of Glandford and Thornage (possibly a mortgage). 1856 Henry Nicholls **16** coal merchant **16**, Ben Nicholls **16** master mariner, John Parker **16** master mariner all of Blakeney.
2 Dec 1867 total loss.

HENRY of Blakeney
55 tons, 55.5 ft, 15.4 ft, 9 ft, built 1786 at Southwick, Sunderland, sloop, running bowsprit.
WSR 11/1843 12 Aug 1843 John Starling **48** and William George Markby Starling **16** master mariner and master both of Blakeney.
20 Apr 1845 sold to Newcastle owners and re-registered there.

HENRY AND ELIZABETH of Cley
162 tons, brig? Master: W Penton [Lloyd's 1834].

HENRY AND ELIZABETH of Cley
80 tons. Master: T Shawl [Lloyd's 1834].

HERO of Blakeney
12 tons, 36.2 ft, 11.1 ft, 5.6 ft, built 1843 by John Richard Raven Richardson (builder's certificate 18 Mar 1843) at Morston, smack, running bowsprit.
SR 6/1843, 8/1844 &16/1852 1 Apr 1843 John Baines **42** fisherman and master of Blakeney and Joseph Raven Richardson **22** fisherman of Morston. 11 Sept 1843 J Baines mortgaged **42** to Martha Cheatle widow of Holt. 11 Dec 1843 J R Richardson sold **22** to William Richardson. 4 May 1844 sold to William Bullen 64 fisherman and master of Blakeney. 22 July 1844 sold **64** to William Dye gentleman of Wells, 11 Dec 1852 W Dye sold **64** to William Hooke fisherman of Blakeney. 2 Nov 1853 W Hooke mortgaged **64** to Robert Daplyn draper of Hindringham for £100+ interest [White's 1844 *Norfolk Directory* Robert Daplyn is listed as victualler at the *Red Lion*].

HEROINE of Burnham Overy
55 tons, 59.6 ft, 14.9 ft, 7.2 ft, built 1851 at Burton Stather by John Wray, Official No. 5105, sloop and ketch after 1882, top up bowsprit, carvel and clench build. Master: John Dunn.
SR 2/1851 28 Feb 1851 Robert Dewing **64** merchant [White's 1854 *Norfolk Directory* coal, corn merchant, shipowner and maltster] of Burnham Overy.
Date unknown when registry cancelled, some time after 1883 converted into lighter.
This billy-boy was built on the Trent by John Wray who was active between 1824 and 1861 [Clapson, 2007: 13-28].

HERBERT (ex **MARCEL**) of Wells
38 tons, 61 ft, 16.3 ft, 7.3 ft, date and place of building unknown.
SR 4/1868 30 Apr 1868 Robert William Elsdon **64** master mariner (and master) of Freeman St. Wells. 29 Oct 1880 R W Elsdon died and **64** left to his widow Emily (also managing owner). 27 Mar 1890 E Elsdon sold **64** to James Gleadhill mariner of Magdalen (?). 19 July 1894 J Gleadhill sold **64** to John Reed farmer and coal merchant of Porlock, Somerset.
19 Dec 1912 registry which remained at Wells cancelled, vessel broken up.

HERO of Blakeney
192 tons, 85 ft, 26.45 ft, 14.6 ft, built 1847 at Venice as **SLAVA**, brig, man's bust figurehead.
SR 4/1865 (transferred from Hull) 11 Apr 1865 Richard Schollar **32** shipowner and James William Mann **32** master mariner both of Blakeney. 11 Aug 1866 R Schollar sold **11** shares to Robert Schollar boatman of Blakeney and 1 Nov 1866 J W Mann sold **24** shares to Robert Schollar. 24 Oct Richard Schollar sold **5** shares to J W Mann and 25 Oct 1867 Robert Schollar sold **40** to J W Mann mortgaged **64** to John & David Morris shipbuilders at Pelaw Main for £512 + 10% interest.
4 June 1868 transferred to Newcastle.

HILARY of Cromer
17 tons, built 1841 by Robert Sunman at Sheringham (builder's certificate 29 Apr 1841), 3 masted lugger, running bowsprit, round stern, clench build.
SR 10/1841 2 Aug 1841 Hilary Nockless **64** fisherman of Cromer.
Oct 1847 run down off Cromer.

HOLKHAM of Wells
80 tons, 62 ft 9 in, 17 ft, 8 ft 6 in, built 1833 by John Parker at Wells, schooner, round stern. Master: H Garratt 1834.
SR 3/1833 19 Mar 1833 Joseph Springall Southgate **64** merchant and Henry Garret **16** master mariner (and master) both of Wells. 4 Jul 1833 J S Southgate mortgaged **48** to Gurney, Birkbeck & Co, bankers of Fakenham. 8 Feb 1834 H Garret mortgaged **16** to Thomas Poolly (probably Pooley or Powley), the same day T Poolly mortgaged **16** to Samuel Bignold gentleman of Norwich (possibly one of the Bignolds associated with the Norwich Union insurance companies). 16 Dec 1834 the same **16** shares transferred to Alexander Gopsill Poolly merchant of Norwich.
16 Dec 1834 J S Southgate and Gurney, Birkbeck & Co transferred **48** to A G Poolly and registry transferred to Gt Yarmouth.
This early shipowning venture by Southgate seems to come unstuck for lack of cash to keep up the mortgage payments

HOPE of Wells
55 tons, 59.4 ft, 17.5 ft, 8.7 ft, built 1803 at Portland, sloop.
SR 7/1860 (transferred from Scarborough) William Smith **64** master mariner of Wells.
3 Apr 1864 lost entering Seaham harbour. You can imagine what a catastrophe this must have been for William Smith who could clearly only afford to buy an elderly vessel and to lose her after only 4 years. One wonders whether he was insured.

HOPE of Wells
120 tons, brig? Master: J Harman [Lloyd's 1834].

HOPE of Blakeney
17 tons, 40 ft, 10.7 ft, 5.4 ft, built 1844 (possibly by John Richardson) at Morston, sloop, running bowsprit.
3/1846 & 3/1854 28 Mar 1846 Thomas Hurn **32** and John Southern **32** shipowners of Blakeney. 9 Mar 1854 both owners sold **64** shares to John Allen gentleman of Wells (20/1836 John Allen listed as mariner).
19 Apr 1856 transferred to Boston.

HOPEWELL of Wells
109 tons, 68 ft 6 in, 19 ft 2 in, 9 ft 4 in, built 1802 at Wells, brigantine. Master: John Curson.
SR 14/1832 & 20/1836 8 Sept 1832 George Crofts **64** merchant [Pigot's 1830 *Norfolk Directory* coal and coal merchant]. 10 Feb 1833 **64** shares mortgaged to John Savory miller of Burnham Overy, discharged 1 July 1833. 18 July 1833 **64** mortgaged to John Woodley, corn factor of Crutched Friars, London, re-registered. 5 June 1840 mortgage to John Woodley discharged. 15 Nov 1841 **64** mortgaged again to John Savory as above.
9 Aug? 1842 registry cancelled, vessel broken up.
Crofts was one the leading Wells merchants but seems to have lived a somewhat hand-to-mouth financial life. John Savory was a frequent lender on the security of ships and John Woodley also lent money to favoured shipowners from time and to time. He also seems to have specialised in the purchase of East Anglian grain. For example, he had dealings with Mingay and Rope at Orford [Stammers, 2008: pp94-7].

HOPEWELL of Burnham Overy
51 tons, dimensions? Built 28 July 1846 by Henry James Tyrrell at Wells, sloop (ketch 9 June 1880), gammon knee.
3 Aug 1846 Thomas Thirtle Mack **22** merchant & farmer of Burnham Thorpe, John Savory **21** merchant and miller at Burnham Overy and James Smith **21** master mariner (and master) of Burnham Overy [additional occupations from White's 1845 *Norfolk Directory*].
August Bank Holiday 1900 a heavy northerly gale caused the **HOPEWELL** (cargo of wheat and oil cake) to drag her anchors and went ashore on the Bar. The lifeboat was towed out by the tug **MARIE** and the crew of three were rescued just as she started to break up [Harman, 1995: 40-1].

HORNSEA of Wells
42 tons, 53.2 ft, 13 ft, 6 ft, built 1836 at Stainforth (on River Don), sloop, topping up bowsprit, clench build, Official No. 4774. Master: Thomas Field 1850.
SR 6/1850 & 3/1851 (re-registered from Goole 43/1839) 18 Mar 1850
William Nettleton Gardner **32** gentleman [1851 Census farmer of 200 acres] of Wells. Robert Garbutt **32** merchant. Another billy-boy sloop and in 1850 *Norfolk Chronicle* she was delivering grain to Leeds and other Yorkshire ports and returning from Hartlepool and Newcastle with coal.
9 Feb 1861 wrecked on Yorkshire.

HULL PACKET of Wells
48 tons, 57 ft, 14 ft, 5 ft 11 in, built 1825 at Louth, sloop, round stern, clench build.
SR 19/1832 28 Sept 1832 John Lubbock **64** shipowner [Pigot's *Norfolk Directory*, shipbuilder]. 30 Apr 1833 J Lubbock sold **64** to Martin Dodman merchant of Thornton [White's *Norfolk Directory* 1844 corn and coal merchant and house at Titchwell where he had a farm].
Re-registered at King's Lynn.
This billy-boy was built at the head of the Louth Navigation connecting the market town of Louth with the Humber at Tetney Haven. Lubbock presumably bought her as a speculation as he soon sold her on to Dodman

HULL PACKET of Blakeney
42 tons, 48.9 ft, 15.3 ft, 7.6 ft, built 16 Oct 1843 (builder's certificate) at Wells by John Lubbock, sloop, running bowsprit. Master: Samuel Daniels 1843.
WS 13/1843 & 9/1859, Thomas William Temple **32** and Charles Temple **32** merchants of Blakeney. 27 Oct 1877 Charles Temple sold **64** to Martin F Page of merchant of Brinton. 27 June 1881 M F Page sold **32** each to W R Smith and Robert Cringle master mariner of King's Lynn.
Re-registered at King's Lynn and wrecked 3 Dec 1894.
A Norfolk billy-boy owned by the biggest shipowners in Blakeney who owned 12 ships between 1839 and 1876 both coasters and deep-sea ships. Page and Turner were their successors. According to the *Norfolk Chronicle*, the **HULL PACKET** was regularly sailing between Blakeney and Hull and was probably one of the vessels on the fortnightly service between her home port and Hull mentioned in White's 1845 *Norfolk Directory*.

HUNTSMAN of Wells
32 tons, 41 ft 2 in, 13 ft 5 in, 6 ft 3 in, built 1832 at Wells, sloop, running bowsprit.
Master: John Smith 1835, James Race 1836, John Watson 4 Dec 1836, William Mason 1 Sept 1836, William Smith 22 Feb 1839, William Kemp 19 Apr 1850 at Goole, John Rix 13 Dec 1861.
SR 5/1835,22/1836 & 9/1845 27 June 1835 Joseph Haycock **32** merchant and William Place **32** master mariner both of Wells. 21 Oct 1837 W Place sold **32** to George Crofts merchant of Wells. 18 Jan 1842 G Crofts sold **32** to Henry John Crofts shipowner of Wells. 28 Nov 1845 Joseph Haycock (late of Wells, now City of London) sold **32** to H J Crofts and the same H J Crofts sold **32** to John Rix master mariner of Wells. 4 July 1853 H J Crofts sold **32** to Leonard Jooby farmer of Pudding Norton.
24 June 1890 sold for breaking up
Sample voyages; 1845 delivered to Wells 15 Mar coal from Goole, 3 May potatoes from Boston, 7 June oats from Boston, 21 June coal from Goole, 5 July coal from Hartlepool. One outward voyage listed in *Norfolk Chronicle* was in ballast but in 1850 she made 2 voyages with grain (6 April and 6 July to Leeds or Wakefield and to 'the Yorkshire Rivers').

INDUSTRY of Wells
87 tons, 61.8 ft, 18.5 ft, 9.8 ft, brig. Master James Powditch 1833.
SR 12/1833 14 Dec 1833 James Haycock (senior) **64** merchant of Wells.
19 May 1836 registry cancelled, broken up.

INDUSTRY of Wells
74 tons, 60.7 ft, 16.8 ft, 9.2 ft, built 1838 by J H Parker at Wells, schooner. Master: Robert Cook 1838, Carter Balls 14 June 1839, Thomas Smith 29 June 1839, James Kew 7 July 1839 and James Powditch 17 July 1840.
SR 10/1838 10 Nov 1838 Thomas Smith fisherman, Robert Munson master mariner, Edward Elliott master mariner and Mary Palmer widow all of Wells and all with **16** shares.
31 Mar 1866 sold to Faversham owner and registry transferred there.

INDUSTRY of Sheringham
41 tons, 45.5 ft, 15.9 ft, 7 ft, built 1842 by Lown & Lown at Sheringham (builder's certificate 20 June 1842), schooner, carvel & clench build. Master: Robert Brocke 1842.
SR 5/1842 24 June 1842 James Breeze **32** and Henry Coleman Pegg **32** both farmers of Sheringham. 7 April 1847 the two farmers sold **32** shares to Robert Cooper Breeze butcher of Sheringham. 26 Feb 1849 R C Breeze now of Bodham mortgaged **32** shares to Thomas Park farmer of Runton on £150+interest. 16 Aug 1850 Thomas Pegg farmer of Sheringham inherited **16** shares from the late H C Pegg.
21 May 1861 sold to Lowestoft owners and re-registered there.
This probably the only cargo ships ever built at Sheringham. Presumably the two original owners had a need to export their grain and to ship in coal.

INDUSTRY of Thornham
30 tons, 54.4 ft, 16.8 ft, 6.6 ft, built 1853 at Tweed (on the S bank of the Tweed opposite Berwick-on-Tweed), sloop, round stern clench build.
SR 3/1865 20 (transferred from Hartlepool) Mar 1865 Martin Dodman **64** merchant of Titchwell and trading out of Thornham. 27 April 1867 M Dodman sold **64** shares to Thomas Alwen, corn merchant of Wells. 2 Mar 1874? T Alwen sold **64** shares to Edward Earle master mariner of Thornham.
2 Sept 1883 foundered off the Lincolnshire coast.

INTEGRITY of Sheringham
21 tons, 41.1 ft, 13.6 ft, 6 ft, built 1838 at Scarborough, yawl, running bowsprit, narrow stern, clench build.
7/1844 (transferred from Scarborough) 1 May 1844 Zacharias Taylor and Edward Brissandon (skipper) **32** each both fishermen of Sheringham.
17 Oct 1854 re-registered at King's Lynn.

INVINCIBLE of Sheringham
26 tons, 49 ft, 13.8 ft, 6.1 ft, built 1844 at Gt Yarmouth, 3 masted lugger, running bowsprit, round stern, clench build.
SR 11/1849 (transferred from Gt Yarmouth 48/1844) 2 Aug 1849 Plane Pegg **64** fisherman and skipper of Sheringham, 3 Aug 1849 **64** shares mortgaged to William Barcham farmer [White's 1844 *Norfolk Directory* freehold farmer & maltster] for £275 (probably the purchase price or most of it).
5 May 1860 registry transferred to Gt Yarmouth .
On the transfer document Pegg signs by his mark and not his signature.

IONIAN of Blakeney
187 tons, 109.9 ft, 23.4 ft, 12 ft, built 1860 at Prince Edward Island, Canada, brig, female bust figurehead.
Master: William Dew
SR 5/1868 4 Aug 1868 Susan Dew **64** shipowner of Salthouse (probably the widow of John Dew, grocer of Kelling Road, Salthouse [Fiddian,2003: 49]). 4 Oct 1878 S Dew died and left **22** shares to William Dew mariner and George Dew labourer **42** both of Salthouse. Manager James Randall (probably of Cley). 27 Sept 1879 G Dew sold **42** shares to William John Dew farm labourer of Salthouse. 13 Mar 1880 W Dew sold **22** to Richard Hay Lynn farm labourer of Salthouse. 5 May1882 these two new shareholders sold all shares to William Crathorne shipowner of Sunderland.

11 Dec 1882 wrecked off Dutch coast
Ships were exported to Great Britain in large numbers from Prince Edward Island. This vessel was too big for local trading. How farm labourers could afford to buy shares in this brig is a mystery.

ISABELLA of Mundesley
72 tons, 56 ft, 16 ft, 9 ft, built 1827 at Newburgh, Aberdeen, schooner. Master: Richard Newton 1840.
SR 8/1840 Francis Wheatley **64** merchant of Mundesley.
10 Feb 1844 registry cancelled, vessel foundered at sea.
Mundesley receives regular cargoes on the beach. There was even a scale of charges for pilotage, ballast, labour etc.

ISIS of Wells
90 tons, 62.8 ft, 18.5 ft 10.1 ft, built 1819 at Wells, brig. Master: John Woods 1833, J Moody 1834.
SR 1/1833 (ex Cley 23/25) 9 Jan 1833 John Lubbock **64** shipbuilder of Wells. 26 Jan 1833 & 3/1834 J Lubbock sold **16** to John Moody mariner of Wells. 3 Apr 1833 J Lubbock sold **16** to William Baker Hazell fishmonger of Dark House Lane, Lower Thames St, London.
15 Mar 1834 J Lubbock sold **16** each to John junior and Charles Lubbock both shipbuilder of Wells.
17 June 1835 all shareholders sold **64** to John Wright Wakefield of N Shields and re-registered at Newcastle.
This brig looks as if it was bought to repair (to provide work for the yard's shipwrights) and then sold on at the earliest opportunity.

JACKALL of Wells
7 tons, 24.6 ft, 9.4 ft, 5 ft, built 1832 at King's Lynn cutter, running bowsprit, clench build.
SR 7/1843 3 Nov 1843 Richard Smith **64** licensed pilot of Wells.
7 Nov 1845 R Smith sold **64** to John Heath fisherman of Brightlingsea, re-registered at Colchester.
According to White's 1845 *Norfolk Directory* there were 8 pilots at Wells including Richard, Edward & John Smith. They would have been licensed by the Corporation of Trinity House of London. Trinity House also maintained a buoy store at Wells. John Heath was probably one of the Essex fisherman who sailed up to North Norfolk to exploit the rich oyster beds.

JACOBINA of Wells or Blakeney
20 ton fishing smack, 4 crew, Official No. 78254.
Transferred from Gt Yarmouth 2/1889.

JAMES AND ANN of Sheringham
28 tons, 45.1 ft, 13.9 ft, 6.3 ft, built 1837 at Gt Yarmouth, 3 masted lugger, running bowsprit, clench build.
SR 2/1847 & 5/1858 3 Mar 1847 William West **32** fisherman and skipper and Henry Pegg **32** husbandman both of Cromer. 17 Jan 1859 H Pegg sold W West **32** shares and he mortgaged **32** shares to R Symonds, shipbuilder of Southtown, Gt Yarmouth on £117 5s, discharged on 11 Mar 1859.
15 Mar 1859 transferred to Gt Yarmouth registry.

JAMES AND ELIZABETH of Wells
30 tons, 38 ft 9 in, 12 ft 8 in, 6 ft 7 in, built 1788 at Queenborough, Kent, smack, running bowsprit.
Master: Thomas Bunn and Frederick Wing 18 Sept 1838.
SR 1/1838 & 5/1839 19 Mar 1838 Edward Lubbock **64** mariner and master of Wells. 18 July 1839 E Lubbock sold **64** to Thomas Dixon Sandling coal merchant of Wells.
14 Apr 1844 T D Sandling re-registered her in King's Lynn and no longer in existence 1865.

JAMES PEAK of Wells or Blakeney
26 tons fishing smack 4 crew, Official No. 14392.
Transferred from Gt. Yarmouth to King's Lynn 8/1887.

JAMES WILLIAM of Wells or Blakeney
24 ton fishing smack, 4 crew, Official No. 60715.
Transferred from Lowestoft 11/1887.

JANE of Thornham
68 tons, 58 ft, 16 ft, 7.9 ft, built at Wells 1844 by John Lubbock, schooner, round stern. Master: William Hendry 1844.
SR King's Lynn 18/1844 Martin Dodman **64** merchant of Thornham.

JANE AND ELLEN of Wells
35tons, 46.5 ft, 14.9 ft, 6.5 ft, built 1839 at Sunderland, sloop, running bowsprit, round stern.
Master: John Hayden 1844, William Edgar Loynes 31 Dec 1845.
WS 5/1844, 12/1847 & 15/1851 (transferred from Maldon 27/1843) William Waters **64** farmer of Wighton. 30 June 1847 lengthened to 55.8 ft, 14.7 ft, 6.3 ft, 91 tons and re-rigged as ketch. 23 Dec 1851 W Waters sold **64** to Robinson Parker merchant of Wells.
10 Oct 1863 sold to W Hartlepool and registry transferred.

JANE MARIA of Cromer
71 tons, 59.6 ft, 15.5 ft, 9 ft, built 1833 at Sutton, Yorkshire, schooner.
SR 17/1840 (transferred from Hull) William Kennedy **23** master mariner and master, John Bayfield **10** tailor both of Cromer, Charlotte Cook **10** spinster of Gt Yarmouth, Henry Harrison junior **21** mariner of Kingsdown, Kent. 11 Feb 1851 J Bayfield sold **10** shares to W Kennedy

Cromer beach 1839 had three sloops discharging coal into farm carts.

8 Mar 1858 re- registered at Yarmouth and still sailing 1865[Clayton].

JASON of Brancaster, Wells and Blakeney
10 tons, 30 ft, 9.5 ft, 5.5 ft, built at Wells 1813, smack, running bowsprit.
Master: Matthew Denton 1843, Stephen Barnstone 24 July 1843.
SR 53/1823, 1/1843, 1/1844 & 4/1851 4 Jan 1844 Stephen Barnstone farmer of Brancaster sold **64** to William Fickling mariner of Brancaster who on 19 Jan 1844 sold **64** to James Fickling master mariner (and master) of Wells. 16 Feb 1845 J Fickling sold **64** shares to William Pells fisherman and skipper of Morston. 12 Dec 1846 mortgaged to Maria Bird spinster of Bodham. 11 Mar 1857 executors of late Maria Bird (William Bird of Hole Hall, Hempstead and Richard Bird of Old Buckenham farmers) sold **64** shares to William Newton master mariner of Wiveton (was this the same William Newton listed in White's 1845 *Norfolk Directory* as a farmer?). 28 Mar 1854 W Newton sold **64** to James High innkeeper of Brancaster.
4 May 1854 vessel sold to another port and registry cancelled.

JASON of Wells
71 tons, 56 ft 9 in, 17 ft 1 in, 7 ft, built 1814 at Barton-on-Humber, billy boy sloop, standing bowsprit, round stern, clinker build.
Master: James Powditch 1834, Elizah Smith 20 July 1837.
SR 4/1834 & 19/1836 1 Apr 1834 Joseph Springall Southgate **64** shipowner of Wells.
8 June 1836 re-measured 54.2 ft, 15.2 ft, 7.2 ft, 18 Mar 1839 lost en route for Newcastle.

JAY of Wells
57 tons, 51.4 ft, 15.5 ft, 9.6 ft, built 1849 ? at Newburgh, Fife, Official No. 14298, sloop and ketch in 1858 at Hartlepool, running bowsprit.
WS 1/1851 transferred from Arbroath 26/1849. John Smith **64** master mariner (and master) of Wells.
1860 lost off Lincolnshire coast.

JEMIMA of Blakeney
15 tons, 37.7 ft, 11.2 ft, 5.2 ft, built 1853 by Joseph Hastings at Gt Yarmouth, Official No. 21233, smack, running bowsprit, clench build.
SR 2/1853 15 Mar 1853 William Warnes **64** fisherman of Blakeney.
2 Mar 1901 registry cancelled, broken up.
Warnes' wife Jemima owned 32 shares in the **LADY CICELY**(1/1846) and no doubt this new vessel was named in her honour.

JESSIE of Wells
146 tons 76 ft, 19.1 ft, 13 ft, built 1839 at New Glasgow, Prince Edward Island, Canada, schooner, female bust figurehead.
SR 9/1849 (transferred from London 257/1846) William Hendry senior **22** shipowner [White's 1845 *Norfolk Directory* master mariner], William Hendry junior **21** both master mariner (and master) and Robert Leeder **21** shipowner (Welland, 62 landlord of the *Sun*, Wells).
1852 sold away from Wells?

JESSIE MARY of Thornham
26 tons, built Forfar 1878 as lugger, later converted to ketch rig and lengthened.
Owned by Nathaniel Woods of Thornham, laid up at Thornham 1914 and may have been converted to a houseboat at Heacham.

JOHN of Blakeney
62 tons, 64.2 ft, 14.7 ft, 8.7 ft, built 1818 at Wells, brig changed 1834 to schooner. Master: William Dean 1846.
SR 10/1846 Robert John Brereton and Randle Brereton **32** each merchants of Blakeney.

JOHN AND ANN of Wells
40 tons, 48 ft, 16 ft, 6 ft, built 1839 at Goole, schooner, round stern, clench and carvel build.
SR 4/1856 (transferred from Boston) James Cook and William Temple **32** each both master mariners of Wells.
2 July 1875 J Cook died and **32** shares inherited by his widow Sarah who on the same day as J Cooks was notified sold her shares as did William Temple to Richard Grainger shipowner of Hull who converted her into a lighter.
Most billy-boys seem to have been sloop or ketch rigged. A schooner of such small tonnage was unusual.

JOHN AND ANN of ?
55 tons, sloop, Official No. 54514, re-registered 5/1867 at King's Lynn, from Goole.
Registry cancelled 31 Mar 1887 after vessel lost.

JOHN AND ELIZABETH
22 tons, 44 ft, 12.4 ft, 6.4 ft, built 1837 at Lowestoft, 3 masted lugger, running bowsprit, clench build.
Master: Thomas Pardon 1850.
SR 9/1850 (transferred from Gt Yarmouth) 29 Apr 1850 Thomas Fiske **64** twine spinner of Syderstone. 11 Apr 1851 W Fiske mortgaged **64** to John Cobb leather seller of Gt Yarmouth on £22+interest and this was discharged on 26 Apr 1852.
12 Feb 1855 re-registered at Gt Yarmouth.
It is unclear whether she fished from North Norfolk. Most of the luggers were based at Sheringham or Cromer and were laid up at Gt Yarmouth in the winter. Syderstone lies inland from Wells and Burnham Overy.

JOHN AND HANNAH'S ENDEAVOUR of Blakeney
59 tons, 53.1 ft, 12.5 ft, 5.7 ft, built 1831 at Leeds, sloop, round stern, topping bowsprit, clench build.
SR 1/1854 (transferred from Goole) 27 Jan 1854 Randle and Robert Brereton **32** each merchants of Blakeney. 29 Oct 1856 Randle Brereton sole owner.
24 July 1858 registry cancelled, vessel lost at sea on passage to Goole.
Another billy-boy built at Leeds like the **JOHN AND REBECCA**.

JOHN AND REBECCA of Cley
36 tons, 56 ft, 14.5 ft, 5.75 ft, built 1849 at Leeds by E & K Teale, sloop, round stern, carvel and clench build.
SR 5/1862 (transferred from Goole) 28 July 1862 James William Porritt **64** shipowner [White's 1864 *Norfolk Directory* merchant] of Cley.
10 Nov 1865 J W Porritt sold **64** shares to John Turner of Catton and John Ellis Turner of Cley both merchants.
20 May 1873 both owners sold **64** to William Hewson merchant of Hull and vessel transferred to Hull.
Page and Turner became the biggest shipowners in Cley and Blakeney in the latter part of the 19th and the early 20th century. Their fleet ranged from an ex fishing smack, to a billy-boy and a small steam coaster.

JOHN AND SUSAN (ex **FERNAND**) of Wells
76 tons, 70.2 ft, ?, 9.4 ft, built at St Malo, France date unknown, schooner.
SR 5/1865 12 May 1865 John Powditch **64** shipowner of Wells [Welland, 49 & 58 innkeeper at the *Red Lion* 1842–1862 and *Ship*, 1857–1865] and foreman shipwright to Henry Tyrrell till 1863 [Stammers, 2011: 38]. 22 Apr 1867 J Powditch died and **64** shares inherited by his widow Susan of 3 Jetty Rd, Gt Yarmouth. 6 Aug 1867 S Powditch sold **64** shares to John Snelling builder of King's Lynn. 15 Jan 1869 J Snelling sold **64** shares Henry Downes publican of King's Lynn. 4 Nov 1872 H Downes sold **64** to William Duffing Jardine shipsmith of W Hartlepool. 23 Nov 1874 W D Jardine sold **64** to John Hammett shipowner of Newport, Mon.
17 Oct 1878 vessel foundered.

JOHN LEE of Cley
66 tons, 62.5 ft, 16.2 ft, 8.5 ft, built 1852 at St Lawrence, Northumbria, schooner later ketch, round stern.
Master: Jeremiah Moore 1852.
SR 17/1852 13 Dec 1852 James William Porritt **32** merchant of Cley and Thomas Sykes shipowner [White's 1854 *Norfolk Directory* merchant's clerk] **32**.
16 Nov 1892 re-measured and re-registered at King's Lynn, lost 29 Nov 1897.
In 1861, **JOHN LEE** made voyages from Newcastle to Hamburg and Konigsberg [Osler, 1998].

JOHN MYERS
75 tons built 1848, schooner.
Owner and master W Burgess **64** of Hunstanton, registered at King's Lynn [Clayton, 1865].

JULIA of Blakeney
23 tons, 39 ft 6 in, 11 ft 10 in, 5 ft 5 in, built 1834 at Barking, smack, running bowsprit, clench build.
SR 3/1843 17 Feb 1843 Kitwood Mann **64** fisherman and skipper of Blakeney.
1866 broken up but registry not closed till 1880.

Barking as a fishing port came to prominence in the 1830s with the Hewett family taking a major role. Many of them fitted out as 'well' smacks and went line fishing for cod off Iceland. The cod were kept alive in the well until their return or transfer to a fish carrier. By the 1840s Barking was beginning to lose to rail connected ports such as Grimsby [March, 1953: 12-16]. The **JULIA** (1834) was another Barking smack owned at Blakeney

JULIA of Wells
78 tons, 62.8 ft, 16 ft, 8.7 ft, built 1843 by Joseph Springall Southgate at Wells, schooner, round stern.
Master: William Smith 1843, John Edwards of Cley 18 Feb 1851.
SR 8/1843 23 Nov 1843 J S Southgate **22** merchant, Abraham Dunn **21** coal merchant and Joshua Johnson **21** innkeeper landlord of the *King's Arms* 1839-1846 [Welland, 2012: 32]. 7 May 1845 A Dunn mortgaged **21** shares to John Savory miller of Burnham Overy, discharged 1 May 1850 and same day sold to J S Southgate. 9 Sept 1853 J Johnson sold **21** shares to J S Southgate.
1875 broken up.
This was the first ship that Southgate after he took over one of the two shipyards at Wells. This was in addition to his multiple interests as a merchant and involvement in the town and harbour administration. The National Maritime Museum owns an engraved rummer with a picture of the **JULIA** and inscribed 'Julia of Wells, Francis Southgate 1854' [Prentice,1994: 14]. This suggests that Francis must have gone to sea possibly as a master before running the Wells Post Office and helping his father.

JULIANA of Wells
36 tons, 54.5 ft, 14.8 ft, 5.5 ft, built 1824 at Hanover, galliot, sliding bowsprit. Master: Thomas Nichols 1850.
SR 5/1850 (not previously registered until decree of the Court of Admiralty 4 Mar 1850). 8 Mar 1850 James Chapman **64** merchant [Whites 1845 Norfolk Directory coal and corn merchant and maltster].
28 Dec 1853 lost off Corton (between Gt Yarmouth and Lowestoft).
Norfolk Chronicle 1 July 1850 sailed from Wells in ballast, no doubt to load coal. Her wreck to the south of Wells suggests that she was on passage for London. It is unclear whether Chapman had kept her off the British Register deliberately. Given there was a decree from the main mercantile court, it rather suggests that was the case.

KATE of Thornham & Blakeney
56 tons, 52.2 ft, 15.1 ft, 7.6 ft, built 1840 by John Lubbock at Wells, sloop, round stern.
Master: Joseph Dix 1840, Samuel Starling 14 Sept 1847, John Coe 28 June 1856.
SR6/1840, 7/1841 & 20/1847 Samuel Sharpe **64** merchant and farmer Sunderland House, Docking. 13 Oct 1847 S Sharpe sold **22** shares to John Harding merchant, **21** to Samuel Harding master mariner both of Blakeney and **21** to John French farmer of Field Dalling.
1875 wrecked.
Given its proximity to Docking, it is probable that the **KATE** traded to and from Thornham between 1840 and 1847. *Norfolk Chronicle* 16 Jan 1850 **KATE** sailed from Blakeney for Goole and 26 Mar for Hull probably with grain cargoes. Later re-rigged as ketch and owned by J Starling of Blakeney [Clayton, 1865].

KATE AND MARY of Wells or Blakeney
16 tons, fishing smack?, Official No. 58373, King's Lynn registry 4/1899.

KATHERINE FRASER of Wells
198 tons, 85.3 ft, 21.3 ft, 11.8 ft, built ? at Newport, Nova Scotia, snow, woman bust figurehead.
SR 21/1847 18 Oct 1847 Richard Lord **64** shipowner [White's 1845 *Norfolk Directory* coal merchant] of Wells.
Sold at date unknown, out of Wells register by 1865.
Many ships were launched on the Canadian eastern seaboard which had been commissioned by British ship brokers or owners or as speculative projects [Ross,1996: 98-117].

KESTREL
20 ton smack. Re-registered from Colchester as 2/1886 of King's Lynn.

KINGFISHER of Blakeney & Cley
15 tons, 38.1 ft, 12.3 ft, 6 ft, built 1823 at Barking, sloop, running bowsprit. Master: William Loades junior 1843.
SR 4/1843 11 Mar 1843 William Loades senior and junior **32** each fishermen of Blakeney. 8 Mar 1851 W Loades senior sold **32** to junior now at King's Lynn.
24 Oct 1853 re-registered at Grimsby.
Barking was a major fishing centre in the early 19th century but lost out to newer ports such as Grimsby by the 1850s. It specialised in well smacks that long lined for prime cod off Iceland and then kept them alive in a wet well to deliver them fresh to market. The **KINGFISHER** and the **JULIA** were two Barking smacks sold to North Norfolk fishermen.

LADY ANNE of Burnham Overy & Wells
76 tons, 62.2 ft, 17.1 ft, 8.5 ft, built 1822 at Wells, brigantine.
Master: W Parker 1834, William Cringle 1836, James Smith 17 Jan 1840, Thomas Luke Harman 1846.
SR 2/1836, 1/1846 & 7/1851 Robert Dewing **64** merchant [White's 1845 *Norfolk Directory* maltster, coal, corn etc at the Staithe] of Burnham Overy. 29 June 1846 R Dewing sold **32** shares each to Francis loose plumber & glazier of King's Lynn and Thomas Luke Harman master mariner (master) of Wells. 31 Jan 1846 the 2 shareholders mortgaged **64** shares to William Harman of Wells on £300+5% interest. 28 Feb 1848 re-registered at King's Lynn. 3 June 1851 William Harman took over ownership with T L Harman remaining as master.
1874 lost.

Wells Quay c.1892 with the **MINSTREL** *alongside. All the quayside buildings were either warehouses or pubs. The* **MINSTREL***'s deck lay-out was simple. She was steered with a big tiller aft; then there was a companion way down to the master and mate's accommodation, a main hatch with a hand winch between the two masts and crew quarters and anchor windlass right up in the bow.*

Thomas Harman was William Harman's brother. William was a master mariner turned shipowner and property owner [Harman, 1995: 4-7]. Her sale was advertised in the 3rd Jan 1846 edition of the *Norwich Mercury*' Sale by private contract Brig **Lady Anne** 75 tons new measurement, loading 100 tons on 8 ft 3 in draught or 525 quarters of barley, price and details from Richard Dewing, Burnham Overy'. This vessel may be named as a tribute to the former Lady Anne Keppel daughter of the Earl of Albermarle and 2nd wife of Thomas Coke. She held the title of Lady in her own right. Her 2nd husband was not created an Earl until 1837

LADY ANNE of Wells
110 tons, 64 ft, 18.4 ft, 10.8 ft, built 1827 at Wells, brigantine.
Masters: R Leeder 1834, Henry Watson 1836, Thomas Hendry, Edward Bunting at Newcastle 18 Sept 1846, William Hendry at Hartlepool 1 Apr 1847, Thomas Crofford (Crawford) 16 Oct 1847, John Hendry at Cley 22 Feb 1850, William Cringle at Hartlepool 21 Apr 1851.
SR 8/1836, 2/1944 & 1/1864 28 Mar 1846 Robert Leeder **64** senior shipowner of Wells and innkeeper at the *Sun* 1812-39 and Robert junior 1839-1865 [Welland,2012: 62]. 19 Jan 1844 R Leeder senior transferred **64** shares to R Leeder junior. 10 Jan 1864 R Leeder junior sold **64** to Joseph Springall Southgate shipowner of Wells. 11 Jan 1868 J Southgate sold **64** to Samuel Tyzack and Jonathon Jopling shipowners of Sunderland, transferred to Sunderland Registry.
This vessel may also be a tribute to Lady Anne Coke.

LADY CICELY of Wells
12 tons, 30 ft, 11 ft, 5 ft, built 1825 at Burnham, Essex, smack, running bowsprit. Master: James Everitt.
SR 3/1842 & 1/1846 18 Apr 1842 Samuel Cable **64** gardener of Wells. 15 Feb 1844 Samuel Cable mortgaged **64** shares to Robert Leeder junior innkeeper of the *Sun*, Wells. 23 Dec 1845 S Cable [now listed as a farmer] and R Leeder junior mortgaged **64** to James Coe the younger of Saxlingham [White's 1845 *Norfolk Directory* farmer] and Jemima Warner (or Warnes) wife of William Warner fisherman of Blakeney. 7 Jan 1846 J Coe junior **32** labourer of Saxlingham and J Warnes **32**.
23 Mar 1854 wrecked at Gt Yarmouth.
This Lady seems to have had no connection with the Cokes.

LAPWING of Wells
72 tons, 58.8 ft, 15.9 ft, 9 ft, built 1849 at Wells by Henry Thomas Tyrrell (builder's certificate 14 Feb 1849), schooner.
Master: James Sturley 1849, Ben Bower 15 Mar 1850, William Hudson 10 June 1852, William Crafer 7 Sept 1853, Edward Bunting 1855.
SR 2/1849 & 3/1855 2 Mar 1849 Henry Tyrrell **64** shipowner [White's 1845 *Norfolk Directory* draper, High St.] of Wells (father of the shipbuilder). 23 Jan 1855 H Tyrrell sold **64** shares to Richard Lord coal merchant of Wells. 25 Mar 1862 R Lord mortgaged **64** shares of **LAPWING** and **WELLS PACKET** for loan of £50 (should this be £500?) + 6% interest from Robert Michael Hammond esquire of Fakenham [White's 1845 *Norfolk Directory*, manager of Gurney's Bank] and Henry Tyrrell of Wells. 17 Mar 1864 transferred to Lowestoft registry as R Lord had moved to Southwold.
5 Mar 1871 sunk in collision in the Dudgeon, 4 crew saved, cited in evidence to *Unseaworthy Ships Commission.*

LAVINIA of Blakeney
64 tons, 59.7 ft, 16.7 ft, 8.9 ft, built 1824 at Gosport, schooner, woman's bust figurehead.
Master: Butcher Starling 1845, William Starling 1850.
SR 5/1845 & 11/1850 3 Apr 1845 John Starling **64** merchant of Blakeney [White's 1845 *Norfolk Directory* also miller]. 31 May 1845 J Starling sold **16** to Samuel Starling and **8** to William Markby Starling both master mariners of Blakeney. 17 May 1850 J Starling **48**, William and Samuel Starling both merchants **8** each. 19 Feb 1853 S Starling sold his **8** shares to W Starling.
Registry closed, abandoned off the Dogger Bank.
The Starlings must have been a close-knit family and one wonders whether Samuel and William had been brought into the landward side of the business in1850. William Starling (senior) had shares in nine ships and there were five other Starlings who had shares in Blakeney ships.

LAVINIA of Blakeney
78 tons, 72.6 ft, 20.6 ft, 9.2 ft, built 1860 at Ipswich, schooner.
SR 3/1860 13 June 1860 John Starling **32** and William Starling **32** merchants of Blakeney, and same day J Starling sold **8** shares to John Howard butcher of Stiffkey and **8** to William Starling Pond ironmonger of Blakeney.
4 July1860 J Starling sold another **8** shares to W S Pond. 16 Aug 1865 all the shareholders sold their shares to a spinster and 2 coal merchants of Arbroath.

LITTLE HELEN of Wells
79 tons, 60.5 ft, 17 ft, 9.7 ft, built 1845 by John Lubbock at Wells, schooner, female head. Master: William Bullard.
SR 7/1845 & 12/1845 28 Aug 1845 Abraham Dunn **64** coal merchant of Wells. 2 Sept 1845 **64** shares mortgaged to John Savory, miller of Burnham Overy and 16 Sept 1845 a second one from the same lender for £170+interest. 8 Dec 1845 A Dunn sold **64** to James Haycock junior merchant of Wells. 9 Dec 1845 J Haycock mortgaged **64** shares + those of the **CAROLINE** to J Savory for £1550+5% pa interest. 17 Sept 1846, another mortgage taken out with Major, Usborne & Kerr, corn factors of London, *Norfolk Chronicle* 8 Nov 1845 sailed from Wells in ballast for Newcastle and 23 Feb 1850 sailed from Wells for Goole with grain, 6 April 1850 arrived at Wells from London with a general cargo.
9 May 1863 stranded at Jutland.

LION of Blakeney
42 tons, lighter?, Official No. 93625, King's Lynn registry 2/1896.

LITTLE MARTHA of Cromer
128 tons, 73.7 ft, 19.8 ft, 11.2 ft, built 1841 at Sunderland, schooner, woman bust figurehead. Master: Francis Park.
SR 12/1841 8 Sept 1841 Mary Smith **15** widow, Thomas Park **37** master mariner both of Cromer and Thomas Emery **12** mariner of Edgefield.
30 Dec 1842 vessel reported lost.

LITTLE POLLY of Wells or Blakeney
17 tons, fishing smack, Official No. 58670, King's Lynn registry1/1897.

LIVORNO of Cley
152 tons, 73.8 ft, 19.9 ft, 12 ft, built 1827 at Wallsend-on-Tyne, brig. Master: Thomas Shawl 1845.
SR 8/1845 (previously also registered at Cley 20 Aug 1838) 28 Nov 1845 Joseph Muskett **21and** William Muskett **21** shipowners of Holt [White's 1845 *Norfolk Directory* grocers and drapers at Market Place, Holt and at Cley], Howard Ramm, and Samuel Bastard **4** each master mariners of Cley and Thomas Shawl **4** master of the *Ship* of Blakeney, and William Muskett shipowner (gentleman) of Attleborough. 28 July 1846 H Ramm, S Bastard & T Shawl mortgaged their shares to the Musketts, discharged 15 Feb 1849. 7 Feb 1849 J Muskett (junior?) of Attleborough, Benjamin Muskett gentleman of Rockland and William Muskett shipowner of Stoke Newington executors of the late W Muskett of Attleborough sold his **6** shares to Colin McCallum, shipbroker of Mark Lane, London. 15 Feb 1849 all shareholders sold the ship to George Cruikshank, coal broker of Aberdeen.
7 Apr 1849 re-registered at Aberdeen.
The land-based Musketts of Holt took majority stakes in 4 ships between 1839 and 1855 but they ensured they had maritime expertise by selling small parcels of shares to 3 local master mariners. And they also persuaded another family member to take a small stake as well. As they had a shop at Cley, they would have been aware of the opportunity to buy this local ship. Her purchase seems to have been more as an investment and not something to aid their existing business.

LIZZIE WATERS of Sunderland
248 ton brig, built 1866 at Hylton, Sunderland, Official No. 47685, owner William Allen of Weybourne [Mercantile Navy List 1872, Mills,1957: 127 painting of LW].

LONDON PACKET of Wells & Cromer
87 tons, 65.4 ft, 16.7 ft, 10 ft, built 1812 at Wells possibly a brig in 1836 and re-rigged as a brigantine by 1842.
Master: Robert London 1836, William Cook 1842.
SR 4/1836 & 8/1842 11 Mar 1836 Robert London **64** master mariner of Wells. 17 June 1836 sold and re-registered William Cook **48** master mariner of Cromer and Thomas Pearson merchant of Sandwich, Kent.
20 Sept 1843 re-registered at Gt Yarmouth.

LONDON PACKET of Blakeney
59 tons, 59.3 ft, 15.4 ft, 7.9 ft, built 18 Aug 1854 by H J Tyrrell of Wells, Official No. 21205, sloop (altered to schooner 18 Apr 1856), running bowsprit.
SR 10/1854 & 10/1859 Thomas William and Charles Temple **32** each merchants of Blakeney. Re-registered 10/1859 Charles Temple sole owner. 27 Oct 1877 C Temple sold **64** shares to Martin F Page and 13 Aug 1882 M F Page to M F Page & E C Turner merchants of Blakeney and Cley [White's 1883 *Norfolk Directory* coal, corn, cake, seed and manure merchants].
22 Dec 1894 lost at Saltfleet, Lincolnshire.
Neither of these two **London Packets** seems to have been a regular service to London!

LORD BYRON of Wells,
109 tons, 71.6 ft, 18.5 ft, 10.6 ft, built 1827 at Wells, brig.
Master: James Powditich 1832, W Parker 1834, James Hayden 1 Dec 1845, Jonathon Elsden 8 May 1849,
Thomas Smith of Cley 15 Dec 1851, James Smith of Cley 10 July 1852.
SR 2/1827 & 2/1840 M Robinson Parker **64** shipowner of Wells [White's 1845 *Norfolk Directory* Lloyd's Agent] who mortgaged all shares to Francis Frowhawk of Houghton farm steward [White's 1845], George Waters of Hindringham [White's 1845 of esquire of Godfrey's Hall] and William Waters of Wighton farmers.
1 Dec 1848 mortgage discharged and a new one agreed with aforesaid and Edmund Kent gentleman of [White's 1845, solicitor of Baron's Hall] Fakenham.
2 Nov 1863 lost on Filey Brigg.
Robinson Parker 1794-c.1865 of East End was a ship's agent, agent for several mutual marine insurance societies as well as Lloyd's and a Harbour Commissioner and the owner of the **LORD BYRON**. *Norfolk Chronicle* 8 Nov 1845 arrived in ballast from Colchester to be overhauled and 6 Nov 1845 sailed in ballast for Newcastle.

LORD COKE of Wells
80 tons, 63.2 ft, 16.4 ft, 9.6 ft, built 1838 by John Lubbock at Wells, schooner. Master: John or James? Place 1839.
SR 4/1839 30 Jan 1839 James Place **32** master mariner of Wells, Thomas Clogg **16** stone merchant and Robert Briggs agent both of Goole. 23 Sept 1841 R Briggs sold **16** to J Place now at Goole. 20 Aug 1842 T Clogg morgaged **16** to John Carter of Knottingley, Grace Gaggs of Pontefract, John Carter & Elizabeth Carter of Howden all common brewers of Knottingley. 8 Apr 1843 T Clogg sold **16** to James Place mariner.
11 Sept 1843 re-registered at Hull (out of Register by 1865 [Clayton]).

LOUISA of Cley
307 tons, 86 ft, 23 ft, 16 ft, built 1823 at Calcutta, barque, woman bust figurehead. Master: Joshua Pallot? 1840.
SR 3/1840 (last registry Hobart, Tasmania) 21 Feb 1840 Joseph **9** and William **10** shipowners of Holt [White's 1845 *Norfolk Directory* grocers and drapers at Holt and Cley], Howard Ramm **3** shipowner of Cley [White's master mariner], Sophia Hawkes **2** and Mary Wright spinsters of Cley, Matthew Joseph Hawkes **2** yeoman of Cley as trustee to Ann Turner wife of George Turner shoemaker of Cley, Clarke Painter **4** [White's glazier and plumber] of Cley, J & W Muskett **3** as trustees for the children of John William Barrell yeoman of Holt, Mary Blomefield **2** widow of William Blomefield yeoman of Barton, George Nurse **2** shopkeeper of Cley, Daniel Newton **4** shipowner of Blakeney [White's grocer], Francis Park **6** master mariner of Cromer, Samuel Smith **3** attorney of Bungay (formerly of Blakeney), William Norman Frost **8** sailmaker of Wapping, London, Samuel Reynolds **4** gentleman of the City of London, 3 June 1844 S Reynolds sold **4** to W N Frost, 12 June 1844 W Muskett sold **1** to W N Frost, 14 Jan 1842 Mary Wright sold **1** to Jeremiah Stangroom tailor of Cley and same day **1** to Mary Ann Moore of Rowhampton, Surrey, 12 Aug 1842 J and M Muskett mortgaged **9** each to Parlett Starling of Norwich as part security on £1500, mortgage discharged 8 May 1844, 1 Now 1843 and 20 May 1844 Joseph Muskett and William Muskett sold **9** each to W N Frost.
What a variety of small shareholders. Given the short time that the managing owners, the Musketts held their shares, it looks as if they may have been out of their depth. W N Frost in London had North Norfolk connections. The **LOUISA** in spite of her age was probably a sound purchase because she was as an Indian-built vessel almost certainly built of teak.

LUCY of Wells
81 tons, 62.2 ft, 8.7 ft, 8.7 ft, built 1811 at Wells, brigantine. Master: Henry Hobart 1836, Wilson Mott 1847.
5 Mar 1836 Samuel Sharpe **64** merchant and farmer of Sunderland House, Docking.
24 Sept 1847 re-registered at King's Lynn (out of Lynn register by 1865).
1834 Lloyd's voyage Dundee to Hamburg.

MADGE
43 tons, steam tug, 5 crew, registered 4/1884 at King's Lynn.
Destroyed by fire 1896.

MAIDEN QUEEN of Wells or Blakeney
26 tons fishing smack, 4 crew, Official No. 56558, King's Lynn registry 4/1891.

MARGARET of Wells or Blakeney
18 tons fishing smack, 4 crew, Official No. 67006, transferred from Hartlepool to King's Lynn 10/1887.

MARIE of Wells
78 tons, 71 ft, 21 ft, 9.4 ft, built 1864 at St Valery, France (10A1) schooner, gammon knee. Master: William Temple 1875.
SR 1/1875 16 Aug 1875 Robert Lombe Carpenter **64** brewer's agent of Wells. 14 Mar 1881 R L Carpenter mortgaged **64** shares to

Frederick John Carpenter brewer of King's Lynn for £528 10s 7d+ interest, discharged 3 Jan 1882. On the same day, R L Carpenter sold **43** shares to F J Carpenter and **21** to Richard Jenkins Sydall, master mariner of King's Lynn.

MARINER'S HOPE of Brancaster & Southwold
50 tons, 60.5 ft, 16.9 ft, 7.5 ft, built 1842 at Wakefield, billy-boy sloop, round stern, clench build.
SR 4/1860 (transferred from Goole) 4 July 1860 Samuel Powditch **48** master mariner and William Powditch **16** mariner both of Brancaster. 2 Aug 1865 W Powditch sold **16** to S Powditch of Southwold (late of Brancaster).
7 Aug 1865 transferred to Lowestoft register.

MARTHA of Wells
13 tons, 34.3 ft 10.2 ft, 5.9 ft, built 1807 at Wells, smack, running bowsprit.
SR 18/1825 & 1/1837 Jeremiah and Robert Lovell **32** each fishermen of Wells.
18 May 1858 registry cancelled as under 15 tons.

MARTHA of Wells
50 tons, 56 ft 10 in, 14 ft 1 in, 6 ft, built 1829 at Wakefield, billy-boysloop, topping up bowsprit, round stern, carvel and clench.
Master: Thomas Harman 1835.
SR 1/1835 William Harman **32** innkeeper of Wells (the *Ship* 1830 and the *Lugger* 1836-39 [Welland, 2012: 38 & 57] and also ship and property owner) and George Wilson **32** coal miner of Silkstone, Yorks. 14 Apr 1836 both shareholders sold **64** shares to John Boothby master mariner of Boston.
21 Dec1836 re-registered at Boston.

MARY of Wells
78 tons, 60 ft 2 in, 16 ft 2 in, 8 ft 9 in, built 1824 at Gt Yarmouth, schooner.
Master: Thomas Hendry 1839, John Edwards 19 Feb 1841, Windham Edwards 2 Apr 1845, Abraham Lawson 15 Feb 1851.
SR 7/1839, 8/1844 & 11/1856 Joseph Springall Southgate **21**, Abraham Dunn **21** both merchants and J H Parker **22** shipbuilder all of Wells. 9 Sept 1841 J H Parker sold **22** to Henry Proudfoot yeoman of Stanhoe and 18 Nov 1843 H Proudfoot sold **22** to J S Southgate. 7 May 1845 A Dunn mortgaged **21** to John Savory, gentleman (miller) of Burnham Overy for £80+5% interest and 2 Feb 1846? a second mortgage to secure £20+interest. 16 Feb 1851 John Savory (with A Dunn's consent) transferred **21** shares to J S Southgate. 1856 (probably) J S Southgate sold **64** to James Sturley coal merchant of Wells (ex master mariner including command of the **COUNTESS OF LEICESTER**). 25 Sept 1856 J Sturley mortgaged **64** shares to J S Southgate for £400+interest.
23 Oct 1857 lost off Aldeburgh?
A Dunn looks to have been in financial trouble as he borrowed such small sums from J Savory and James Sturley was a master mariner before coming ashore and the £400 mortgage probably represents the sale price of the **MARY**.

MARY of Cley
153 tons, 75.6 ft, 21 ft, 12.6 ft, built 1837 at Blyth, brig.
SR 1/1871 William Mann **64** master mariner of Cley.
18 Dec 1876 condemned and broken up.
She carried 240 tons of coal and regularly trade from the North East ports to London or France. Wages per month in 1870 £8 master, £5 mate, cook £3 12s, seaman £3 [Mellor, 1992: 31-2].

MARY of Wells
c.50 tons, 58.1 ft, 13.7 ft, 6.5 ft, built 1842 at Wisbech, sloop re-rigged as a ketch 1859, top up bowsprit, round stern, carvel and clench build. Master: R Cringle 1855.
SR 9/1855 9 Apr 1855 (purchased from William Andrson, Bainford, Durham) William Cooke **64** coal merchant of Wells, 28 Mar 1861 deceased and his shares inherited by his widow Sarah. 2 Sept 1862 Sarah Cooke sold **64** shares to Sarah Crofford (Crawford), widow of Wells. 10 Feb 1863 S Crofford died and her **64** shares transferred to her executors: Charles Edward Bull Collector of Customs and Thomas Garwood junior solicitor both of Wells. 10 Feb 1867 C E Bull & T Garwood mortgaged **64** to Charles J Beeching & Robert Leamon shipbuilders of Wells for loan of £23 4s 7d +5% interest. Discharged at date unknown and 23 May 1867 Bull and Garwood sold **64** to John Phillip Fox master mariner of Wells.
It looks as if the loan from the shipbuilders was to cover the cost of repairs they had carried out on the vessel. It seems strange that two professionals could not come with sufficient cash.

MARY ANN of Wells
36 tons, 52.2 ft, 12.7 ft, 5.4 ft, built 1812 at Boston, sloop, topping up bowsprit, round stern, clench build. Master: William Denson 1836.
SR 7/1836 23 Mar 1836 William Spooner **64** merchant of Wells.
27 Oct 1855 registry cancelled, vessel lost about 10 years previously!

MARY ANN of Wells
69 tons, 69.3 ft, 16.3 ft, 8.6 ft, built 1838 by J H Parker at Wells, schooner, round stern. Master: Joseph Loynes 1838.
SR 8/1838 & 11/1855 Robert Thurston Loynes **64** gentleman of Wells [White's 1845 *Norfolk Directory* attorney of the Buttlands, Wells].
15 Oct 1853 re-registered at Woodbridge? 18 Jan 1860 R L Loynes sold **64** to Joseph Springall Southgate shipowner and merchant of Wells, Jan 1868 J S Southgate sold **43** to Francis Southgate merchant (son) and **21** to J Parker master mariner both of Wells.
Broken up 1875.
This shows the attractiveness of shares in ships to local residents when a professional like Loynes was prepared to buy a new vessel and presumably run with her master's assistance for 22 years.

MARY ANN of Blakeney
47 tons, ketch built 1832, re-registered 1/1885 at King's Lynn from Gt Yarmouth (15/1863) and owned by Edward C Turner of Blakeney.

MARY ANN of Mundesley
56 tons, 53.6 ft, 17.1 ft, 8.1 ft, built 1847 at Sunderland, schooner.
SR 13/1852 (transferred from Sunderland 23/1848) 1 Sept 1852 John Kirk **32** farmer and William Kirk **32** master mariner both of Mundesley. 4 May 1850? J & W Kirk mortgaged **64** shares to Thomas Pearce and Thomas Thackray timber merchants of Sunderland. 4 May 1862 transferred to Lowestoft registry.
1865 master and owner W Clark - could that be a mistake for Kirk? [Clayton, 1865].

MARYLAND
? tons, schooner or ketch, 4 crew, registered as 1/1884 at King's Lynn.
Lost 22 Nov 1897.

MAY of Sheringham
12 tons, 33.4 ft, 10.3 ft, 5 ft, built 1832 by Robert Sunman at Sheringham, 3 masted lugger, round stern, clench build.
SR 16/1840 20 July 1840 John Cooper **64** fisherman of Sheringham.
15 Mar 1850 registry cancelled as under 15 tons.

MIDAS of Wells or Blakeney
22 tons, fishing smack, Official No. 53328, King's Lynn registry 1/1896.

MIGNONETTE of Blakeney
182 tons, 110.8 ft, 21.6 ft, 12.3 ft, built date and port ?, brig, woman bust figurehead.
SR 5/1863 15 Mar 1863 David Thomas **64** master mariner of Blakeney. 11 May 1863 D Thomas sold **4** to Charles Temple merchant and **2** to Charles Johnson Temple shipowner both of Blakeney and **24** to Alfred Bencke merchant of London. 12 May 1863 D Thomas sold **6** to Henry George Yates merchant of London and **10** to William Patrick farmer of Glenton, Northumberland. 14 June 1863 D Thomas sold **8** to Thomas Smirke shipowner of Newcastle. 29 Mar 1864 D Thomas sold **8** to T N Temple, shipowner probably of Blakeney.
13 Dec 1864 lost at Mogador, Morocco.
Thomas off-loaded 60 shares to his associates. The number of shareholders and their places of residence shows how wide a North Norfolk shipowner's contacts could be. This ship probably never visited her home port but like most of the bigger ships owned in Blakeney cross-traded and her wreck at a Moroccan port is evidence of that.

MINERVA of Wells
89 tons, 63.1 ft, 17.2 ft, 11.1 ft, built 1841 at Belle Port Inverness, schooner, female bust figurehead.
SR 12/1853 (transferred from Inverness 32/1841) William Newsom senior **48** shipowner [White's 1845 *Norfolk Directory* master mariner] and William Newsom junior **16** master mariner (and master).
3 Mar 1854 registry cancelled vessel and her papers lost.
Norfolk News 14 Jan 1854 the **MINERVA** lost on Thornham beach after her anchor parted, William Newsom, Henry Boxall (mate) and 4 crew drowned.

MINSTREL of Wells
59 tons, 57.3 ft, 15.3 ft, 8.4 ft, built 25 Aug 1847 by Thomas Henry Tyrrell, Official No. 21217 at Wells, schooner, scroll figurehead.
Master: Henry Howell 1847.
SR 17/1847 & 3/1869 4 Sept 1847 Thomas Thirtle Mack **64** shipowner & farmer of Burnham Thorpe. 16 Sept 1869 John Savory **32** merchant & miller and managing owner of Burnham Overy and Henry Howell **32** master mariner and master. 9 Dec 1891 H Howell sold **16** shares to J Savory and **16** to William Temple, master mariner.
May 1904 stranded at Chapel Lincs and broken up
One of the best known Wells-built schooners as she was photographed in Wells and at Blakeney, and she was shown in frame in the model of Tyrrell's shipyard.

MIRANDA of Blakeney
187 tons, 85 ft, 23.0 ft, 14.1 ft, built 20 Apr 1847 at Newcastle, brig, female figurehead.
SR 6/1858 29 June 1858 Benjamin Nicholls **64** master mariner of Blakeney. 30 June 1858 William Jarvis Boyce **11**, James Parker **10**, William Schollar **21** all master mariners of Blakeney and Douglas Cooper **11** shipbuilder of Newcastle.
Sold or lost sometime before 1865.
As with **MIGNONETTE** the original purchaser off-loaded the majority of the shares and as these transactions took place the day after registration, they must have been agreed before hand.

MIRANDA
20 ton fishing smack, registered 12/1882 at King's Lynn, Official No. 864.

MORNING STAR of Brancaster
21 tons, 36 ft 6 in, 11 ft 11 in, 5 ft 11 in, built at Scarborough 1835, smack, running bowsprit, clench build, deck cabin forward.
SR 15/1852 (transferred from Scarborough) 3 Dec 1852 Robert Simmons **64** fisherman and skipper of Brancaster.
1863 condemned.

MYSTERY of Wells
114 tons, 75.4 ft, 18 ft, 10.7 ft, built 1851 by J S Southgate at Wells, schooner. Master: Francis Southgate 1851, Temple 1864.
SR 12/1851 16 Sept 1851 Joseph Springall Southgate **64** shipowner, shipbuilder and merchant of Wells. 21 Jan 1854 **64** shares mortgaged to Gurney, Birkbeck & Co, bankers of Fakenham 'to secure payment and balance of account'.
18 Oct 1884 sold to Goole owners and re-registered there.
Shipping & Mercantile Gazette 10 June 1864 arrived at Wells from Swansea (probably with anthracite for the maltings).

NANCY of Wells
54 tons, 56.2 ft, 11.5 ft, 8.3 ft, built 1787 at Ipswich, schooner.
SR 2/1842 (transferred from Faversham 10/1826, 31 Apr 1842 John Haydon **64** master mariner and master of **NANCY**.
1 Sept 1842 wrecked and broken up. Let's hope Haydon was insured.

NAOMI of Brancaster
36 tons, 54.4 ft 12.6 ft, 5.6 ft, built 1839 at Lincoln, sloop, round stern, carvel and clench build.
SR 5/1861 5 Sept 1861 (transferred from Gt Yarmouth) Thomas Winterbone senior and junior **32** each both mariners of Brancaster.
22 Oct 1880 registry cancelled converted into lighter.
A billy-boy well suited for trading to and from Brancaster.

NAR
139 ton brig, re-registered at King's Lynn 31/1884 and transferred 27Apr 1898 to Glasgow.

NELSON of Wells
21 tons, 35 ft, 12 ft 9 in, 5 ft 9 in, built 1807 at Wells, sloop, lowering bowsprit (same as topping up), re-rigged 1836 as smack with running bowsprit. Master: Edward Smith 1833-38, Thomas Walker 26 Dec 1838 at Wells, William Smith 16 Aug 1841 at Wells.
SR 4/1833 & 26/1836 4 Apr 1833 James Smith **64** fisherman of Wells. 30 Dec 1836 Thomas Smith **64** fisherman of Wells. 30 Aug 1838 Thomas Smith transferred **16** each to Richard Smith and Edward Smith both fishermen of Wells.
1855 lost at Brancaster.

NELSON of Wells
20 tons?, 33 ft, 12 ft 1 in, 5 ft 1 in, built 1823 at King's Lynn, smack, clinker built. Master: James Reed 1834.
SR 5/1834 29 Mar 1834 J H Parker shipbuilder **32** and John Powditch **32** shipwright both of Wells. 7 Mar 1835 J H Parker sold **32** to J Powditch and 4 Dec 1835 J Powditch sold **64** to John Gilbert Wardell mariner of King's Lynn. 5 Dec 1835 J G Wardell mortgaged **64** with J Powditch on £15+5% pa interest. Presumably re-registered at King's Lynn.
It looks as if the shipbuilder and the shipwright bought her to renovate and sell on. Powditch later ran pubs in Wells as well as acting as foreman shipwright at Tyrrell's yard.

NELSON of Wells
64 tons, 57 ft 4 in, 16 ft 1 in, 8 ft, built 1825 at Wells, sloop, hoist up bowsprit (same as a topping up bowsprit), round stern.
Master: Thomas Powditch 1832.
SR 41/1825, 13/1832 & 18/1832 19 Apr 1832 Joseph Springall Southgate **64** merchant of Wells transferred **64** shares to Hannah Southgate, widow of Wells, and 10 Aug 1832 she mortgaged **64** shares to Gurney, Birkbeck & Co, bankers of Fakenham for £550+interest. 9 Sept 1832 re-registered with J S Southgate as sole owner. 16 Dec 1834 Gurney, Birkbeck & Co foreclosed on mortgage and sold **64** shares to Alexander Gopsill Poorly or Pooley merchant of Norwich who re-registered **NELSON** at Gt Yarmouth.

NEPTUNE of Brancaster and Thornham
16 tons, 30 ft 10 in, 11 ft 8 in, 5 ft, built 1823 at King's Lynn, sloop, running bowsprit, clench build.
George Sheldrake **64** master mariner of Brancaster.
1 May 1843 G Sheldrake sold **64** shares to John Crane, miller of Thornham and 13 June 1843 transferred to King's Lynn register.
A very small billy-boy ideal for Thornham.

NEW BUXTON of Wells
21 tons, 42 ft 2 in, 13 ft 1 in, depth of hold, built 1849 by Henry Hastings, 3 masted lugger, running bowsprit, clench build.
SR 10/1849 Henry Nickels **64** fisherman (and skipper) of Wells. 1871 registry transferred to Gt Yarmouth.

NEWCASTLE PACKET of Blakeney
54 tons, 57.8 ft, 15.5 ft, 8 ft, built 1849 by Thomas Claxson at Blakeney, schooner, running bowsprit. Master: John Parker 1849.
SR 12/1849 & 2/1866 William Cooke **32** of Glandford and Robin Cooke **32** of Thornage both millers. 9 Mar 1866 re-registered with the same shareholders. 12 Mar 1874 R Cooke of Thornage sold **32** to Robert? Cooke of Glandford.
12 Nov 1889 broken up at Blakeney [Hooton, 1996. 260].
Norfolk Chronicle 1850 12 Jan sailed for Newcastle, 23 Feb arrived from Newcastle, 2 Mar sailed for Newcastle, 16 Mar arrived from Newcastle. On the this slim evidence, it would seem she was on a regular packet service to Newcastle.

NEW DART of Sheringham
24 tons, 25 ft? (more likely 45 ft), 13.1 ft, 6 ft, built 1830 at Lowestoft, 3 masted lugger, running bowsprit, clench build.
SR 11/1844 & 12/1850 16 July 1844 Eliner Breeze **22**, Christopher West **21** and Edmund West **21** all fishermen of Sheringham and EW skipper. 13 Feb 1850 C and E West sold **42** shares to Robert Cooper Breeze, butcher of Bodham. 15 Mar 1850 E Breeze innkeeper and fish merchant and R C Breeze mortgaged **64** shares to Mrs Martha Cheatle of Holt [White's 1845 *Norfolk Directory* has her

as notable resident – a wealthy widow perhaps] for £90+5% pa interest. 4 Apr 1850 the Breezes took out a second mortgage with Thomas Park gentleman of Runcorn? (more likely to be Runcton or Runton) for £75+5%. 24 May 1850 R H Hooper **64** (mortgages discharged?).
1869 broken up.

NEW EAGLE of Brancaster
48 tons, 54.5 ft, 13.3 ft, 6.4 ft, built 1849 by Thomas Green at York, sloop, top up bowsprit, carvel and clench build.
Master: Ellery Emerson 1840.
SR 8/1850 & 6/1862 22 Apr 1850 Martin Dodman **64** shipowner of Brancaster. 26 Aug 1862 M Dodman sold **32** to Ann Rix (or Dix) widow and John Southerland **32** master mariner both of Brancaster. 21 Nov 1863 A Rix sold **32** to Edward Henry Southerland master mariner and Henry Herring carrier both of Thornham. 20 Apr 1864 J Southerland sold **16** each to H Herring and William Allen innkeeper both of Thornham.
3 Feb 1886 sold to Grimsby owners.

NEW HENRY of Sheringham
12 tons, 33 ft, 10.8 ft, 5 ft, built 1839 at Sheringham, 3 masted lugger, running bowsprit, round stern, clench build.
SR 9/1839 7 Oct 1839 Emmanuel Middleton **32** fisherman and skipper, James Middleton **16** fisherman both of Sheringham and Edward Bayfield **16** fisherman of Beeston. 18 Jan 1850 E Middleton sold **5** to J Middleton.
6 Feb 1860 registry transferred to Gt Yarmouth.

NEW HILARY of Cromer
20 tons, 39.8 ft, 13.2 ft, 6.1 ft, built 1848 by Henry Hastings at Gt Yarmouth, 2 masted lugger, running bowsprit, round stern, clench build.
SR 7/1848 & 5/1851 Henry Nichels **64** fisherman and skipper of Cromer. 19 May 1851 re-registered after being altered and enlarged.
11 Aug 1865 transferred to Gt Yarmouth.

NEW HOPEWELL of Wells
65 tons, 60 ft 10 in, 17 ft 5 in, 8 ft 8 in, built 1834 at Wells, schooner. Master: David Archer 1836.
SR 6/1834, 16/1836, 7/1837 & 2/1839 2 June 1834 Matthew Curson **32** master mariner (and ship's master) of Wells and James Allesbrook **32** tanner of Worthing, Norfolk [White's 1845 *Norfolk Directory* in partnership with Robert Hart tanner, fellmongers, wool and timber merchants]. 4 June 1834 M Curson mortgaged **32** shares to John Savory miller of Burnham Overy for unspecified amount. Re-registered 16 Apr 1836. 1 Jan 1838 M Curson's mortgage discharged and he sold **32** shares to J Allesbrook who then mortgaged all his **64** shares to J Savory. Jan 1839 J Allesbrook sold **64** to Michael Robinson Parker merchant of Wells.
22 Jan 1840 lost in gale.

NEW LOTTERY of Sheringham
10 tons, 31 ft, 10.9 ft, 4.9 ft, built 1828 at Gt Yarmouth, Official No. 6918, 3 masted lugger, running bowsprit, round stern, clench build.
SR 9/1844 26 July 1844 John Cooper **64** fisherman of Sheringham.
16 Mar 1850 registry cancelled as under 15 tons.

NEW WALTER AND ANN of Sheringham and Wells
30 tons, 51.2 ft, 14 ft, 6.7 ft (or later 53 ft, 15.8 ft, 6.5 ft), built 1840 at Gt Yarmouth, 3 masted lugger, clench build and converted to ketch c.1879.
SR 14/1850 & 1/1879 15 July 1850 Christopher West **64** fisherman & skipper of Sheringham. 17 July 1879 William Temple **64** master mariner (also master and managing owner) of Wells although Hooton stated she was working to and from Blakeney and was a converted herring drifter [Hooton, 1996: 252].
18 Dec 1903 registry cancelled, broken up.

NILE of Wells
120 tons, 79.1 ft, 21 ft, 11.2 ft, built 1859 by Joseph Springall Southgate at Wells, brigantine.
SR 3/1859 5 Mar 1859 J S Southgate **64** shipowner, shipbuilder & merchant of Wells. 18 Jan 1860 J S Southgate transferred **64** to Robert Thurston Loynes solicitor of Wells, possibly a mortgage because R T Loynes re-sold or returned **64** shares 6 May 1861. 27 Sept 1861 J Southgate sold **32** shares to John Savory merchant of Wells (miller of Burnham Overy?). 27 Sept 1863 J Savory died and his shares left to his wife and 2 sons and 23 Dec 1863 late J Savory's share sold back to J S Southgate. 28 Nov 1864 J S Southgate off-loaded all **64** shares to the following residents of Wells: Francis Southgate **16** gentleman, Richard Oldham **8** master mariner, Richard Cawdron **4** pilot, Robert Plattin **4** printer, Francis Burnham Southgate **4** postmaster, John Powditch **4** foreman shipwright, John Shreeve **4** shipwright, Hammond John Parker **4** master mariner,
James Elenor **4** shipwright, Edward Bailey Baines **4** master mariner, John Coe **4** master mariner, John Loynes **4** master mariner. There seems to be a gap in Transactions between 1864 and 1868 as some new names turn up as shareholders after the latter date. 6 Aug 1868 Susan Powditch (probably daughter of J Powditch) **4** shares which she on her marriage passed on to her husband James Snelling, merchant of King's Lynn. 20 Sept 1869 E B Baines died and left **4** to his widow Phoebe Baines. 12 Apr 1871 W Green died and left to his widow Mary Ann Elizabeth Green of Wells. 13 Nov 1875 Hammond J Parker sold **2** to Thomas Hayhow master mariner of Wells. 20 Jan 1876 James Elenor sold **2** to J Loynes and 15 Feb 1878 Edward John Matson sold **2** to J Loynes. 25 Mar 1877 J Loynes sold **8** to William Temple master mariner of Wells. 1 Dec 1879 James Snelling sold **4** to W Temple. 18 Dec 1882 Robert Plattin died and his **4** shares went to his executors Ann Mary Plattin his widow and Alfred Pumphrey grocer of Hunstanton. 20 Mar 1869 John Ramm died leaving **2** to his widow Ann Maria Ramm. 8 Sept 1883 Francis Southgate sold **16**, Robert Oldham **6**, Richard Cawdron Smith **4**, John Plumb Ramm **2** and Francis Burnham Southgate **4** to Dixon Taylor Sharper, sailmaker of W Hartlepool.

According to Lloyd's 1883 register F Southgate was managing owner. 13 to 19 Sept 1883 and 4 Oct 1883 remaining shareholders sold out to D T Sharper. 3 Nov 1884 D T Sharper sold **21** to Samuel Matters of W Hartlepool and 10 Sept 1886 **20** shares (worth £60) to J Pattison shipwright of W Hartlepool. 28 Sept 1886 J Pattison sold **10** to S M I Matters master mariner of Ipswich.
8 Dec 1886 stranded on Redcar Rocks and lost.
This multiple ownership of small numbers of shares was unusual in North Norfolk though common in other coastal ports e.g Portmadog or Pwthelli in North Wales. The **NILE** was the last commercial ship to be built in Wells for local owners. A declining number of vessels were bought in the 1860s and all were second hand.

NORFOLK TAR of Wells
103 tons, 68.6 ft, 17.3 ft, 11.1 ft, built 1848 by Thomas Henry Tyrrell at Wells, certificate 11 May 1848, Official No. 24573, schooner, male figurehead.
Master: Robert Claxton 5 June 1848, Robert Ince Jan 1849, Robert Kew 25 Mar 1850 and Stephen Simmons 27 Apr 1853.
SR 5/1848 13 Apr 1848 Henry Tyrrell (father) **16** merchant, Thomas Powditch **16** [Whites 1845 *Norfolk Directory* master mariner], John Powditch **16** shipowner, shipyard foreman and landlord of the *Red Lion* [Welland, 2012: 48] and William Newman Frost **16** sailmaker of 2 Globe St, Wapping, London.
1870 re-registered at Lynn .
Lloyd's List 11 Jan 1850 arrived at Dublin from Alicante (fruit cargo?), 16 May reported in the Danish Sound on passage from Riga to Liverpool, 11 July 1850 arrived at Fleetwood from Riga (timber and timber products?). The **NORFOLK TAR** like some other bigger North Norfolk ships tramped from port to port and was not employed on the coastal grain and coal runs. Frost, the London sailmaker, made investments in other Norfolk ships including the 3 masted barque, **GUADALETE** which he had built by Thomas Tyrrell at Wells.

NYMPH of Brancaster
45 tons, 59.5 ft, 16.2 ft, 6.9 ft, built 1828 at Gainsborough, billy-boy sloop, round stern, carvel and clench. Master: James Smith 1862.
SR 4/1862 (transferred from King's Lynn) 5 July 1862 James Dix **64** master mariner of Brancaster, 6 Mar 1866 J Dix transferred **64** shares to James Joseph Dix master mariner of Brancaster and 25 June 1867 J J Dix sold **64** to James Chapman merchant of Wells.
15 Oct 1869 wrecked at Heacham.

OCEAN of Wells
79 tons, 62 ft, 16 ft 11 in, 8 ft 7 in, built 1831 at Wells, sloop. Master: Robert Watson 1832.
SR 16/1832 22 Sept 1832 John Chapman **64** merchant of Wells and the same day mortgaged **64** shares to Gurney, Birkbeck & Co of Fakenham. 11 Nov 1834 J Chapman and his bankers sold **64** on to Francis and George Bean merchants of Norwich (mortgage cancelled 13 Nov 1834). Registry transferred to Gt Yarmouth and bought by the London, Lowestoft, Beccles & Norwich Shipping Co for their weekly packet service between London and Norwich [Malster, 1871:17]. *Norfolk Chronicle* 23 Feb 1832 auction of ships at Wells, auctioneer William Spelman at the *Crown*, Wells, Lot 11 '*Fast sailing sloop* ***OCEAN*** *78 tons launched at Wells August 1831, well adapted for the coal and corn trades and carries 550 quarters of barley on 7 feet 1 inch, copper fastened up to the main wales*'.
John Chapman stayed in shipowning despite this set back. He wholly owned the **WHEATHIILL** until 1840, the **STAG** 1840-63, the **ALBION** 1843-45 and had a part share in the **ADVANCE** 1833-35. All these vessels were mortgaged at some point. The **OCEAN** was stranded off Eyemouth on passage to Sunderland with coal and salt, her crew of 3 were saved [*Commission for Unseaworthy Ships*, 1873].

OCEAN CHILD of Wells
121 tons, 77 ft, 18.1 ft, 11 ft built 26 Apr 1853 by J S Southgate, schooner. Master: James Kew 1853.
SR 7/1853 1 June 1853 Joseph Springall Southgate **64**, merchant, shipowner and shipbuilder of Wells.
30 Jan 1858 sold to John Rawling, Daniel King and William Smith of London (merchants?), and re-registered there. Southgate may have had built her speculatively and did not find her a buyer until 1858. It was not uncommon for shipbuilders to operate their own products until they could find a buyer.

OCEAN WAVE of Wells
63 tons, 58.4 ft, 15.2 ft, 7.7 ft, built 1852 by Henry Thomas Tyrrell at Wells, sloop, round stern. Master: John Watson 1852, Mussett 1864.
SR 10/1852 2 July 1852 Henry Tyrrell of Wells shipowner and John Powditch shipwright **32** each both of Wells.
1873 lost.
It is unclear which Henry Tyrrell took the shares but it was probably Henry Tyrrell senior, the grocer and draper, High St, Wells. John Powditch was H T Tyrrell's foreman also ran the *Red Lion* and had shares in several other ships [Stammers, 2011: 38]. *Shipping & Mercantile Gazette* 7 June 1864 **OCEAN WAVE** arrived at Newcastle, 27 June 1864 arrived at Wells from Seaham (coal?).

OLIVE BRANCH of Wells
42 tons, 75.3 ft, 15.2 ft, 8.46 ft, 26 HP, built 26 Jan 1857 at N Shields, paddle tug, sloop, round stern, clench build.
SR 1/1867 (transferred from N Shields) 22 Mar 1867 James Arthur Beeching **64** shipbuilder of Wells. 11 April J A Beeching sold **21** to Frederick & George Smith merchants of Wells [Pigot's 1869 *Norfolk Directory* maltsers at Wells and E Dereham], **21** to Robert Leamon shipowner of Whitwell [White's 1864 *Norfolk Directory* tanner of Whitwell Hall] and **22** to John Louis Marriott merchant of Narborough [White's 1864 maltster, coal and corn merchant at Narborough and with premises with his partner Robert Marriott on the Quay at Wells]. 26 Jan 1869 R Leamon sold **11** shares to the Smiths and **10** to J L Marriott.
1878 broken up in Dover harbour by A Verey & Co engineers and contractors.
Beeching was acting as agent and probably surveyor for the 3 subsequent owners. All three merchant firms had a definite interest

Blakeney Quay c.1900 with the **MINSTREL** *again lying off the main quay with another topsail schooner behind her. She was quite tubby lines designed for cargo carrying not speed.* **CK81** *is a Colchester registered oyster dredging smack. The rich offshore oyster beds attracted both local smacks and those from elsewhere, with the Essex boats leading the way. Note the granaries running down to the Quay in the background.*

in a good tug for the port. The tug **ECONOMY** which arrived at Wells in 1840 was approaching the end of her working life, and was broken in 1870.

ORION of Wells
72 tons, 55 ft 10 in, 17 ft 6 in, 9 ft 1 in, built 1825 at Whitby, schooner.
Master: Isaac Sturley 1834, James Sturley 1836, William Cook 22 Sept 1838, James Smith 14 Dec 1838, William Hudson 16 Oct 1839.
SR 7/1832, 9/1836 & 3/1838 9 May 1834 Joseph Springall Southgate **64** merchant of Wells [Pigot's 1830 *Norfolk Directory* coal & corn merchant the Quay], re-registered 9/1836, 5 Apr 1838 J S Southgate sold **64** shares to George Crofts merchant of Wells [Pigot's 1830 maltster] and the same day G Crofts mortgaged **64** shares to J S Southgate, discharged 15 Nov 1841 and on the same day G Crofts sold the vessel to J Savory miller of Burnham Overy.
13 Dec 1842 registry cancelled, vessel wrecked.
Possibly the same **ORION** which was sold by the London, Lowestoft, Beccles & Norwich Shipping Co. [Malster,1971.17].

ORKNEY LASS of Wells
319 tons, 109.2 ft, 26.2 ft, 16.2 ft, built 1849 at Stromness, Orkney, 3 masted barque, woman figurehead.
SR 9/1858 18 Oct 1858 (transferred from Liverpool) Joseph Haycock **44** coal & corn merchant of Wells and John Powditch **20** innkeeper at the *Red Lion* and foreman shipwright. Same day J Powditch sold **20** to J Haycock. 20 Oct 1858 J Haycock sold **21** to William John Sturley master mariner of Burnham Westgate. 28 Feb 1861 W J Sturley sold **16** to Arnold George master mariner of Llys-frane, Pembrokeshire, and same day A George mortgaged **16** shares for £250+5% interest, discharged 23 July 1863.
1860 lost off Brest.
Almost certainly never visited her home port, her previous owners (T & J Harrison of Liverpool) had been trading her between Liverpool and Brazil and once owned a painting of her.

OSBORN AND ELIZABETH of Cley
179 tons, 91.5 ft, 23.5 ft, 13.1 ft, built 11 June 1857 at Ramsgate, brig, female figurehead.
SR 2/1867 13 Apr 1867 William Allen **64** shipowner of Weybourne. 17 Apr 1867 W Allen sold off small parcels of shares to the following: **3** to Henry Benjamin Mason master mariner, **6** to William Lown butcher both of Cley, and Richard Funnell accountant of Holt, **4** to William Cooke gardener of Weybourne, **5** to James Jary shipowner of S Shields, **10** to Samuel Tipping innkeeper of London and Phillip Allen farmer of Cley. 14 July W Cooke sold **3** to Elizabeth Clarke married woman of Langham.
18 Sept 1873 lost at Hango, Finland.
Lloyd's register had H B Mason as master in 1869 and her last voyage from Newcastle to France. Mason would have managed the

technical side for Allen. The shareholders in S Shields and London suggest these were business contacts and Jary seems to have been a N Norfolk name.

OSPREY of Wells
109 tons, 71.66 ft, 22.2 ft, 10.8 ft built 1863 at Nantes, France, schooner, scroll figurehead.
SR 1/1870 9 Dec 1870 John Plumb Ramm **12** innkeeper of the *Red Lion* 1862-1906 [Welland, 2012:48] and managing owner, William Staines Andrews **9** merchant's clerk, Robert John Shreeve **9** shipwright, Richard Smith **9** pilot, James Chilvers **9** merchant's clerk, James Sayer Howard **6** shipwright all of Wells. 24 Apr 1871 J Chilvers sold **9** to J P Ramm. 31 Oct 1876 W S Andrews sold **9** to J P Ramm. 26 Sept 1879 J S Howard sold **6** to James Smith junior mariner of Wells. 24 Nov 1880 all remaining shareholders sold **64** to Isaac Jackson shipbroker of Goole.
3 Dec 1880 re-sold her to Richard Earnshaw shipowner of Goole. Re-registered at Goole.

OUSE of Wells
123 tons, 68 ft 7 in, 21 ft, 10 ft 5 in, built at Thorne 1794, brig. Master: J Wright 1833, William Hendry 1834.
SR 2/1833 , 10/1834 & 10/1836 28 Feb 1833 Francis Wright **64** merchant of Wells and on same day sold **32** to William Hendry, master mariner of Wells. Re-registered 31 July 1834 unspecified alteration in her design F Wright listed as mariner. 14 Apr 1836 same owners F Wright now resident of Liverpool.
17 June 1836 registry cancelled, broken up.

OVERY PACKET of Wells
63 tons, 57 ft, 15.6 ft, 9 ft, built 1839 by J H Parker at Wells, schooner.
SR 6/1839 Richard Dewing **64** merchant of Wells although the Register stated he was a Wells resident White's 1845 *Norfolk Directory* listed him as a maltster, coal, corn etc merchant of Burnham Overy Staithe. This ties in with the vessel's name.
23 Mar 1866 lost near Colchester.
She may have been on a regular run to London, the *Norfolk Chronicle* of 18 Jan 1845 reported her arrival at Wells 'with goods'.

PALMERS of Bacton
74 tons, schooner. Master and part owner: George Smith of Bacton.
3 crew from Bacton or Walcott, a regular collier for Walcott.
1873 sold to William Starling of Blakeney, 9 Aug 1873 3 month round trip to Baltic. Later on regular coal run from Newcastle to Blakeney. Still registered 1899 [Malster, 1995:7].

PARAGON of Sheringham
28 tons, built 1844 at Gt Yarmouth, Official No. 6745, lugger.
SR 6/1846 (transferred from Gt Yarmouth) Henry West senior and junior **32** each fishermen of Sheringham with junior as skipper.
15 Apr the Wests sold **32** shares to Loads West fisherman of Sheringham.
Sept 1884 wrecked and sold by auction June 1885 registry cancelled.

PARTHENIA of Cley
184 tons, 90.5 ft, 23.6 ft, 13.4 ft, built at King's Lynn, snow, female bust figurehead.
SR 6/1861 12 Nov 1861 William Allen **32** farm bailiff of Weybourne, William Dixon **16** farmer of Weybourne and James Jary **16** master mariner of Cley. 2 Dec 1878 all shareholders sold vessel to Bessey & Palmer, shipowners and coal merchants of Gt Yarmouth. According to the Norfolk Shipping Exhibition in 1957, the figurehead of this vessel was displayed in the Castle Museum, Norwich. See also **ALSWOLD, LIZZIE WATERS** and **WILLIAM AND JOHN**.

PATRIOT of Blakeney
45 tons, 71.7 ft, 16.2 ft, 7 ft, built at S Shields 1861, paddle tug, sloop, round stern, clench build.
SR 2/1877 10 Feb 1877 Martin Fountain Page **64** merchant of Brinton near Holt. 3 Aug 1882 M F Page sold **64** M F Page & Edward Clifford Turner (as the firm Page & Turner) merchants and shipowners of Blakeney.
26 July 1896 Page & Turner sold **64** to the Pendennis Co, Dock Chambers, Sutton Bridge, Lincs who in 1897 sell on to Newcastle owners. There is a painting of the **PATRIOT** registered as a fishing boat ***LN74*** [Hooton, 1995: 254]. Paddle tugs had been used for trawling.

PEARL of Wells and Blakeney
138 tons, 74.9 ft, 20.3 ft, 13.5 ft, built 1826 at Southtown, Gt Yarmouth, snow, female bust figurehead.
SR 3/1858 (transferred from Liverpool) 19 Mar 1858 Joseph Haycock **32** merchant and shipowner of Wells and John Cademy **32** master mariner of Cley (also master). 24 Jan 1866 J Haycock sold **32** to Robert Vince shipowner of Blakeney. 23 Feb 1867 R Vince sold **32** to J Cademy and 12 Oct 1867 registry to Lowestoft
Lloyd's Register 1869 last voyage Newcastle to the Baltic.

PECHERIES FRANCASISES No 17
Fishing vessel transferred to King's Lynn 1/1886.

PEGASUS of Cromer
222 tons, 88 ft 2 in, 23 ft 11 in, 6 ft 3 in, (last measurement is suspect, 16 ft more likely), 3 masted ship, half sham stern galleries and female bust figurehead.
SR 2/1841 23 Mar 1841 William Cook **48** and William Jarvis Cook (and master) both master mariners of Cromer, 29 May 1841 the Cooks mortgaged **64** shares to Samuel Bignold esquire of Norwich for £850+interest. Bignold was a major figure in Norwich as secretary of the Norwich Fire & Life Insurance Societies.
27 June 1846 re-registered at Newcastle.

PETREL of Wells
124 tons, 78.2 ft, 18.5 ft, 10.9 ft, built 1845 Picton, Nova Scotia, Official No. 6302, brig, scroll figurehead. Master: William Ballard.
SR 13/1850 (transferred from Caernarfon 21/1849) 2 July 1850 John Crawford **32** fisherman, Jonathon Shreeve **16** ship carpenter and innkeeper at *Jolly Sailor* 1845-1864 [Welland, 2012; 31] and Robert Crawford **16** fishermen all of Wells.
6 Dec 1858 sold and re-registered at London.

PHANTOM of Blakeney
104 tons, 77.2 ft, 19.6 ft, 11.85 ft, built 1845 at Prince Edward Island, Canada schooner, female bust.
1/1861 (transferred from Sunderland) 25 Feb 1861 Robert Mustens **8** merchant of Newcastle, William Nurse **48** mariner (and master) of Blakeney and William Ward Nurse **8** shipowner of Blakeney. 17 Dec 1861 R Mustens sold **8** to W W Nurse and 28 Mar 1862 W W Nurse sold **16** to W Nurse.
29 Oct 1862 abandoned in sinking state off Jutland. This suggests she was trading to the Baltic or N Germany. PEI built many ships for British owners.

PLANET of Wells or Blakeney?
50 tons, sloop?, Official No. 4817, 1864-1893 on King's Lynn Register as Wells or Blakeney owned and transferred to Hull 1893.

PIONEER of Wells or Blakeney
28 tons, fishing smack, Official No. 89042, King's Lynn registry 2/1897.

PREMIER of Cley
12 ton lugger, Official No. 21260, 3 crew.
SR Cley 4/1838
Broken up?

PRIMROSE of Cley
112 tons 70 ft 8 in, 19 ft 3 in, 12 ft 1 in, built 1816 at Saltcoats, Ayrshire, brigantine.
7/1852 31 Mar 1852 William Maycombe Gibbs the elder **27** coal merchant and William Henry Gibbs **27** master mariner (and master) both of Cley, and Thomas Lynes **10** gardener of Kelling.
17 Apr 1853 transferred to Ipswich (presumably sold to Ipswich owners).

PRINCESS VICTORIA of Wells
85 tons, 63 ft 2 in, 17 ft 5 in, 9 ft 7 in, built 1835 by John Lubbock at Wells, schooner.
SR 9/1835 28 Sept 1835 John Lubbock **64** shipbuilder of Wells.
21 Oct 1835 sold to London owners and registry transferred there.
She was clearly built as a speculation by Lubbock who was lucky to find a buyer quickly.

PROSPECT of Blakeney
225 tons, 94.9 ft, 24.9 ft, 14.9 ft, built at Sunderland 1853, snow, gammon knee figurehead. Master: G Boyce 1880s.
1/1866 (transferred from Sunderland) 30 Mar 1866 William Isaac Bensley **64** master mariner of Blakeney and master of **PROSPECT**. 14 June 1866 W I Bensley sold **26** to William Lown, butcher of Clay and 29 May 1866 another **6** to Edward Jervis master mariner of Clay.
25 Jan 1883 missing since this date.
Lloyd's register voyages between Newcastle and Baltic.

PROSPEROUS FRIENDS of Cley
10 tons, lugger, Official No. 6921, 3 crew, registered at Cley 12 Aug 1838.
Broken up 1970.

PROVIDER of Wells
67 tons, 78.1 ft, 16.7 ft, 9.5 ft, built 1870 at N Shields, paddle tug, sloop, clench build.
SR 1/1877 (transferred from Harwich) John Lewis Marriott **32** maltster, coal & corn merchant at Wells and Narborough, and Frederick & George Smith **32** malsters and merchants at Wells, Scarning near E Dereham and Gt Ryburgh.
18 Aug 1888 all shareholders or their executors sold **64** to Nathaniel Hoppin steamship owner of Sunderland and registry transferred to S Shields.
Bought as a replacement for **OLIVE BRANCH**.

PROVIDENCE of Wells
103 tons, 65 ft 9 in, 18 ft 9 in, 10 ft 4 in, built 1835 by J H Parker at Wells, brigantine. Master: Carter Balls.
SR 4/1835 18 June 1835 J H Parker **64** shipbuilder of Wells, and same day mortgaged her to Robert Sillett the Younger, wine merchant of Fakenham [White's 1845 *Norfolk Directory* listed a Robert Sillett as a hop & seed merchant and one –possibly the senior as a gentleman both of Broad Street] to secure £116+interest. 29 Oct 1835 J H Parker and R Sillett sold **64** to James Eddy, William Warren and John Raymond Trustees of the Truro Shipping Co, Truro.
J H Parker had built the **PROVIDENCE** without a buyer and needed a loan to tide him until a sale could be effected.

PROVIDENCE of Sheringham
31 tons, 51.5 ft, 14.2 ft, 6.8 ft, built 1851 at Gt Yarmouth, 3 masted lugger, running bowsprit and clench build.
SR 11/1851 12 Aug 1851 Henry West senior and junior **32** each, fishermen of Sheringham with junior as skipper.
21 May 1868, sold and transferred to Gt Yarmouth.

PROVIDENCE of Blakeney
15 tons, 35.4 ft, 11.8 ft, 5.9 ft, built 1852 by John Hastings at Wells, Official No. 21231, smack, running bowsprit, clench build.
SR 3/1852 18 Mar 1852 William Lincoln **64** master mariner of Blakeney.
1882 registry closed vessel under 15 tons and sailed exclusively in Wells Bar.

PRUDENT of Blakeney
44 tons, 44 ft, 17 ft, 7.9 ft, built 1801 at Cowes, Isle of Wight, sloop.
SR 6/1856 Randle Brereton **64** merchant of Blakeney. 6 Feb 1860 mortgaged with other vessels for loan of £2000 from Harvey's Bank, Norwich.
31 Dec 1863 broken up.

QUEEN VICTORIA of Burnham
7 tons, 25 ft, 9.4 ft, 4.9 ft, built 1838 at Wisbech, smack.
SR 2/1838 & 4/1838 5 Apr 1838 William Amiss **64** mariner of Burnham (Overy?).
1869 broken up.

Wells Quay c.1910, with a local ketch and beyond a steel three-masted schooner and a boomie (ketch-rigged) Thames barge.

RAMBLER of Wells
148 tons, 88.7 ft, 22.1 ft, 11.8 ft, built 1856 by J S Southgate at Wells, snow.
SR 7/1856 16 Aug 1856 Joseph Springall Southgate **64** merchant, shipbuilder and owner of Wells, 22 Apr 1857 J S Soutgate sold **64** to Joseph Haycock merchant of Wells. 21 Feb 1866 J Haycock sold **21** to Robert William Elsden master mariner of Wells. 29 Dec 1866 J Haycock sold **43** to William Jecks timber merchant of Beccles.
23 Jan 1867 lost on Happisburgh Sand.
Norfolk Annals 1850-1900 the **RAMBLER** was launched by Miss Ellen Rump daughter of a local surgeon at Southgate's yard. 10 Aug 1861 **RAMBLER** arrived at Konigsberg with 244 (long) tons of coal from Newcastle, gross freight £77.63. Also made a trip from Newcastle to Rouen the same year [Osler, 1998].

RAPID of Brancaster
14 tons, 31 ft, 10 ft 8 in, 4 ft 10 in, built 1805 at King's Lynn, sloop, running bowsprit, clench build.
SR 12/1834 & 8/1834 2 July 1832 Mathew Springall **64** fisherman and skipper of Brancaster. 7 July 1834 sold to Robert Skipper (skipper) and William Springall **32** each and both fishermen of Brancaster.
24 Apr 1843 registry cancelled, wrecked and broken up at Snettisham.

REBECCA AND ELIZABETH of Mundesley
60 tons, built 1845, schooner.
Registered at Lowestoft, owner and master William Kirk or Mundesley [Clayton].
The master/owner was presumably related to the Kirks who were farmer and merchants at Mundesley.

REFUGE of Sheringham
14 tons, 34.1 ft, 11.4 ft, 5 ft, built 1840 at Sheringham by Roger Sunman, 3-masted lugger, running bowsprit, round stern, clench build.

SR 15/1840 & 4/1847 21 July 1840 Robert Cox **64** fisherman and skipper of Sheringham. 22 Mar 1847 **64** transferred to Richard Cox junior fisherman of Sheringham.
1869 registry closed as under 15 tons.

REGENT of Cley
73 tons, schooner? Master: W Green [Lloyd's 1834].

RESOLUTION of Cley
51 tons. Master: W Gibbs [Lloyd's 1834].

RESOLUTION of Cley
39 tons, 54.4 ft, 12.9 ft, 5.4 ft, built 1836 at Knottingley, billy-boy sloop, top up bowsprit, round stern, clench and carvel build. Master: John Bell 1853.
SR 6/1853 13 May 1853 James William Porritt **42** merchant of Cley and Eleanor Pegg **22** widow of Holmfirth, Yorkshire (seems unlikely; Pegg is a Norfolk surname. What took her to Holmfirth?)
1970 registry closed, broken up.

RIGA of Cley
177 tons, 88.3 ft, 23.4 ft, 14.6 ft, built 1846 at Dundee, brig, female bust figurehead.
SR 7/1859 (transferred from Dundee)16 Apr 1859 James William Porritt **64** shipowner and corn merchant of Cley. 7 Apr 1859 J W Porritt transferred **22** shares to William Dixon shipowner (farmer?) of Weybourne. 3 June 1859 J W Porritt transferred **8** shares to David Porritt gentleman of Norwich.
15 Apr 1874 sold to Swedish owners.
A name like **RIGA** suggests she was designed for the Baltic trade.

ROBERT AND CATHERINE of Wells
75 tons, 60.6 ft, 16.2 ft, 9 ft, built 1837 by John Lubbock of Wells, schooner. Master: James Cook 1853.
SR 6/1837 & 8/1853 7 Dec 1837 Robert Leeder senior **32** shipowner (landlord of the *Sun* 1812-1839) and Robert Leeder junior victualler (*Sun* 1839 – 1865) [Welland, 2012: 62] and William Newsom **16** master mariner and master all of Wells. 27 April 1853 R Leeder junior and Thomas Leeder executors of the will of R Leeder Senior sold his **32** shares to John Howard butcher of Stiffkey. 5 Nov J Howard and R Leeder sold ship to King's Lynn and re-registered there.

ROKEBY of Blakeney
202 tons, 83.3 ft, 20 ft, 14.2 ft, built 1844 at Hull, Official No. 25318, snow, woman bust figurehead. Master: Thomas Starling 1852.
SR 4/152 (transferred from Newcastle) 24 Apr 1852, Charles Temple **16** merchant, David Thomas **16** master mariner, Bartholomew Jary **8** farmer all of Blakeney, Thomas Smirke **12** coal dealer and William Patrick **12** butcher both of Newcastle. 30 Apr 1852 C Temple sold **4** to Charles William Cooke surgeon of Cley.
Sold 1856?
Surgeon Cooke was doubtless related to Cookes the millers at Glandford and Thornage.

ROLLA of Cley
116 tons, brig?
Master: J Mann [Lloyd's 1834].

ROSALIND of Newcastle
74 tons built 1853 schooner owner by W F Windham, gentleman of Felbrigg Hall [Clayton, 1865].

ROSE IN JUNE of Blakeney
18 tons, 32 ft 2 in, 11 ft 7 in, 5 ft 11 in, built 1824 at Blakeney, smack, running bowwsprit.
SR 2/1842, 1/1845 & 18/1847 28 Feb 1842 Reuben Boyce **64** fisherman & skipper of Blakeney. 1 May 1843 R Boyce sold **32** to Elizabeth Agnes Rush widow of Cley. 15 May 1843 R Boyce sold his other **32** to William Bastard fisherman & skipper of Blakeney. 6 Mar 1847 E A Rush sold **32** to Thomas Bainbridge fisherman of Blakeney. 14 Sept 1847 W Bastard sold **32** Thomas Bainbridge fisherman & skipper of Blakeney. 1 May 1854 T Bainbridge sold to James Richardson fisherman of Burnham Overy.

ROSE IN JUNE of Blakeney
17 tons, 36.3 ft, 11.9 ft, 6.5 ft, built 1837 at Blakeney, smack, running bowsprit.
SR 22/1847 5 Nov 1847 John Cotts Howes **48** farmer of Saxlingham and Michael Loads **16** fisherman and skipper of Blakeney.
11 Apr 1865 registry cancelled, transferred to King's Lynn.

ROSE IN JUNE of Wells
40tons?, 49 ft, 16 ft, 6 ft?, built 1843 at Wakefield, sloop, round stern, carvel and clench.
SR 1/1856 (transferred from Goole) John Bransford **32** master mariner and John Crawford shipowner [Craven's 1856 *Norfolk Directory* fish merchant, the Quay] both of Wells. Feb 1861 John Crawford transferred **32** shares to Susan his wife. 12 Mar 1864 Susan Crawford sold her **32** shares to John Powditch foreman shipwright and landlord of the *Red Lion*, Wells. 24 Mar 1864 J Powditch mortgaged **32** for £110+5% interest with William Edward Loynes solicitor of Wells, discharged 10 Dec 1864. 10 Dec 1864 J Powditch & J Bransford mortgaged **40** shares to Joseph Haycock merchant of Wells for £140+interest.
7 Dec 1867 lost at Barrow Gap, Holkham, the crew of 3 managed to hang in the rigging even though the hull had been parted in two until a crab boat, the **PET**, had been brought doen to the beach and rescued them. The Stacey brothers and the two other members of the crab boat's crew were awarded £5 for this brave act [Harman, 1995:23].

ROVER of Wells
14 tons, 35 ft, 9 ft 11 in, 5 ft 6 in, built at Boston 1828 (or 1831), smack, running bowsprit, Official No. 21247.
Master: William Bacon 1834, Christopher Cook 1 Mar 1844, George Green. also 1841 John Crawford owner.
SR 11/1834 & 2/1841 16 Sept 1834 John Shreeve **64** ship carpenter of Wells. 11 Mar 1841 J Shreeve sold **16** each to John and Robert Crawford fishermen of Wells.
29 Mar 1850 registry cancelled as under 15 tons.

ROYAL ALBERT of Cley
48 tons, 60 ft, 10 ft?, 6 ft, built 1839 at Knottingley, Official No. 4755, sloop, round stern, carvel and clench build.
SR 2/1856 John Porter and Peter Porter **32** each both master mariners of Cley.
28 Dec 1858 lost at Gravelines.

ST HILDA of Wells
92 tons, 61.6 ft, 18.3 ft, 11 ft, built 1841 at Sunderland, schooner, female bust figurehead. Master: William Hudson 1853.
SR 11/1853 (transferred from Hartlepool 10/1845) 30 Sept 1853 Mary Hudson **64** widow of Wells and same day mortgaged to William Elgar draper & grocer of Wells for £500+interest [Craven's 1856 *Norfolk Directory* lists him as a gentleman at the Buttlands].
16 Apr 1863 M Hudson and William Crafer of Faversham transferred registry to that port.
Crafer is a north Norfolk name and Mary Hudson must have sold him half her shares some time before this change. Mary Hudson signed with an X, while Crafer wrote his full name.

SAFE AND SATISFACTORY of Cley
12 tons, lugger, Official No. 73137, 3 crew.
Registered at Cley 16/1837 (later taken off as under 15 tons).

SALLY of Wells
15 tons, 33.9 ft, 11.7 ft, 6.5 ft, built 1845 at King's Lynn, cutter, running bowsprit, clench build.
Master: Lewis Stacey 1846, John Fiddy 1852.
SR 5/1846, 6/1852 & 2/1869 (transferred from King's Lynn 19/1845) 25 Feb 1846 William Dye **64** mariner of Wells. 28 Feb 1852 sold to John Fiddy fisherman (and skipper) of Wells. J Fiddy at some earlier date sold **32** each to Nathaniel Isaacks and William Guild both fishermen of Wells. 12 June 1869 N Isaacks & W Guild mortgaged **64** shares to D? Chapman merchant of Wells for £50+5% interest and same day Chpman transferred the loan to the National Provincial Bank at E Dereham; mortgage discharged 13 Oct 1870. 15 Oct 1870 N Isaacks mortgaged **32** to Richard Smith pilot of Wells for £30+5% interest and discharged 23 Dec 1873 only to be renewed the same day with R Smith for £20+5% interest. 26 May 1878 W Guild died intestate and also his widow 'in straitened circumstances'. 16 Dec 1879 the late W Guild's **32** shares transferred to Robert William Guild fisherman of Gt Grimsby. 27 Feb 1873 N Isaacks transferred his **32** shares to William Isaacks ropemaker of Wells. 6 Apr 1894 W Isaacks sold **64** Shares to Samuel Hibbert fisherman of Wells.
5 May 1900 broken up.

SALLY AND ELIZABETH of Runton
12 tons, 33.2 ft, 11.2 ft, 5 ft, built 1834 at Ludham, 3 masted lugger, running bowsprit, round stern, clench build.
SR 10/1843 (transferred from Gt Yarmouth 20/1841) 25 July 1843 Thomas Edwards **64** fisherman and skipper of Runton.
23 May 1847 registry cancelled as under 15 tons.

SAMUEL of Cley
76 tons, 60.5 ft, 16.7 ft, 8.8 ft, built 1791 at Gt Yarmouth, schooner.
SR 13/1853 (transferred from Gt Yarmouth 14/1844) 29 Oct 1853 David Parlett **64** mariner and master of Salthouse. 29 Oct D Parlett sold **16** shares each to Stephen Ampleford, innkeeper [Craven's 1856 *Norfolk Directory* beer retailer and brewer] and William Davison farmer both of Cley and Thomas Dew shepherd of Salthouse.
Out of register by 1865.

SAMUEL AND SARAH of Cley
156 tons, 79.85 ft, 23.45 ft, 13 ft, built 1 June 1838 at Sunderland, brig.
SR 9/1857 & 1/1868 (transferred from Sunderland) 24 July 1857 James Randall **64** shipowner (& master) of Cley, and same day J Randall sold **9** to Thomas Lynes gardener of Kelling, **8** to Osborne Springfield gentleman & merchant of Catton, **7** to Richard Shore innkeeper of Gt Yarmouth and **8** to Clarke Painter yeoman of Cley. 22 Jan 1868 O Springfield sold **8** to J Randall and 24 Jan 1868 re-registered with James Randall described as managing owner and the same shareholders.
26 Jan 1871 run down off Cley.
As with the **SAMUEL** above and other local ships, you find a master/managing owner who is able to sell most of the shares to friends, relations of business associates. In the case of the **SAMUEL AND SARAH**, they must have received some return on their investment to hold it for 13 years. Parlett

SAMUEL ENDERBY of Blakeney
404 tons, 108.3 ft, 29.3 ft, 19.3 ft, built at W Cowes, 3 masted barque, male bust figurehead.
SR 4/1858 (transferred from London) 4 Apr 1858 Charles Temple **12**, Thomas William Temple **20** merchants, Thomas John Starling **10** master mariner all of Blakeney, William Patrick **11** butcher of Newcastle and William Farquaher **11** optician. 12 May 1858 all shares sold to William Beatson ship joiner of Rotherhithe.
25 June 1870 broken up.

This odd combination of shareholders (who got them together? The Temples?) only retained ownership for a month. It must have been a speculative purchase or perhaps made and then finding the vessel needed unaffordable repairs.

SARAH of Cley
98 tons, 64.8 ft, 17.8 ft, 9.7 ft, built 1813 at Gt Yarmouth, Official No. 25396, schooner.
SR 14/1851 27 Nov 1851 John Porter **64** master mariner (and master) of Cley.
29 Nov 1859 ship lost, master drowned – information from John I Brown agent for Eliza Porter, the widow.

SARAH of Wells
81 tons, 62 ft 9 in, 17 ft 1 in, 8 ft 5 in, built 1833 by J H Parker at Wells, schooner, round stern.
Master: James Sturley (later of the **COUNTESS OF LEICESTER**) 1833.
SR 8/1833 21 Aug 1833 Joseph Springall Southgate **48** merchant and J H Parker shipbuilder both of Wells. 5 Feb 1834 J S Southgate and J H Parker sold all shares to the Trustees of Norwich & Beccles Shipping Co. Registry transferred to Gt Yarmouth
A speculative building by Parker to keep his shipwrights in work. The Norwich & Beccles Shipping Co was the same as the London, Lowestoft, Norwich & Beccles Shipping and Trading Co which was established with the opening of the new harbour at Lowestoft and the New Cut between the Rivers Waveney and the Yare in 1833. They advertised a weekly service between London and Norwich [Malster, 1971;17].

SARAH of Wells
77 tons, 65 ft 9 in, 16 ft 10 in, 8 ft 5 in, built 1835 by J H Parker at Wells, schooner, round stern. Master: C Balls.
SR 8/1835 19 Sept 1835 Carter Balls **64** master mariner of Wells and same day mortgaged to J H Parker for £325+interest. 6 Jan 1836 J H Parker mortgaged **64** shares held as security for C Balls' loan to secure £200+interest from William Gilham timber merchant of Fakenham. 29 Apr 1836 C Balls took out a second mortgage on **64** shares for £65+interest with William Newman Frost sailmaker, East Middlesex. 22 July 1836 William Gillham took out a second mortgage on **64** shares with Robert Sillett [White's 1845 *Norfolk Directory* Robert either a gentleman or a hop and seed merchant] for £142 2s 3d +interest. 20 Dec 1836 W Gillham and R Sillett took a mortgage on **64** shares with the East of England Bank, Fakenham, to secure the balance of W Gillham's account £79 9s 5d. 28 Nov 1837 East of England Bank transferred **64** shares to J H Parker.
11 Dec 1837 sold to Liverpool owners and re-registered there.
What a trail of indebtedness, it is unclear whether or not the older mortgages were discharged but the Bank seems to have put the title in Parker's hands in order to effect her sale. Notice that William Frost the London sailmaker was involved.

SARAH of Wells
78 tons, 63.1 ft, 16.6 ft, 9.4 ft, built 1845 by Thomas Henry Tyrrell at Wells, schooner. Master: Robert W Hammond.
8/1845 12 Sept 1845 Joseph Springall Southgate **32** and Thomas Garwood **32** gentleman [White's 1845 *Norfolk Directory* attorney of the Buttlands] both of Wells. 21 Jan 1853 T Garwood sold **32** to J S Southgate. 11 July 1853 J S Southgate sold **64** to William Gibbs of Harding, Hampshire. Lloyd's List 17 May 1850 arrived at Wells for shelter bound for Goole.

SARAH AND ANN of Wells
30 tons, 42.7 ft, 12.2 ft, 7.7 ft, built 1842 at Sunderland, sloop, running bowsprit.
SR5/1842 12 July 1842 Robert Middleton **64** master mariner (and master) of Wells. 6 Sept 1842 possibly sold to King's Lynn owners and certainly re-registered there.
This was a brand new sloop. Was Middleton acting as agent for someone?

SARAH REBECCA (ex **GIROFLEE**) of Blakeney
85 tons, 70.8 ft, 19.8 ft, 9.5 ft, date and place of build unknown, schooner.
SR 3/1868 7 Apr 1868 James Hurn **64** master mariner (and master) of Morston. 19 Apr 1868 J Hurn sold **12** to John Hewitt mariner of Morston. 11 Jan 1869 the 2 shareholders mortgaged **64** shares to Samuel Arnold farmer of Bale for £150+interest and this was discharged 14 Sept 1874. (some transactions may be missing) 30 Aug 1881 J Hewitt mortgaged **12** shares to J Hurn for £35+ 5% interest and 28 Aug 1882 J Hurn sold **64** shares to James William Hewitt mariner of Blakeney and the same day mortgaged to J Hurn for £150+5%. Re-registered at King's Lynn 9/1882 and by 1884 converted into a lighter.

SAUCY LASS of Wells
74 tons, 68.8 ft, 16.8 ft, 9.1 ft, built ? schooner, female bust figurehead. Master: William Crafer 1855.
SR 1/1855 11 Jan 1855 John Massingham **64** shipowner [White's 1854 *Norfolk Directory* cooper].
13 Mar 1856 registry transferred to new volume, p.15 (no sign of this in main register), and may have been transferred to another register.

SEA of Cley
220 tons, 81.4 ft, 22.9 ft, 15.2 ft, built 1837 at Sunderland, brig. Master: Peter Kitwood 1844.
SR 5/1844 (transferred from Sunderland) 12 Apr 1844 William Newton **64** gentleman of Wiveton [White's 1844 *Norfolk Directory* - farmer]. 1 May 1844 W Newton sold **64** shares to Thomas Twedle Drysdale, shipowner of Hartlepool and 2 Feb 1852 re-registered at that port.
Newton had in effect lent his money while Drysdale raised the funds for her purchase. One wonders what the connection was between Newton and Drysdale was. There was no third party broker. Possibly Drysdale sold coal to North Norfolk customers.

SEA FLOWER of Blakeney
113 tons, 73.1 ft, 19.2 ft, 11 ft, built 1840 at Ipswich, schooner, female bust figurehead, Official No. 17650.
SR 2/1854 Isaac Mann **16**, Samuel Daniel **16** and William Isaac Bensley **16** (master) all mariners of Blakeney, and John Daniel **16** shepherd of Stiffkey.
1879 broken up.

SEAFLOWER of Brancaster and Wells
49 tons, 58.6 ft, 13.6 ft, 6.6 ft, built 1842 at Wakefield, sloop, topping–up bowsprit, round stern, carvel and clench build.
Master: William Jeckling 1844, Henry Crafer 23 Dec 1844, John Cringle 23 Apr 1853.
SR 10/1844 & 7/1858 (transferred from Wisbech) 23 Mar 1844 William Jeckling **64** shipowner and also master of Brancaster. 23 Jan 1845 **32** shares transferred to William Spooner merchant of Wells and returned to W Jeckling 13 Dec 1845. 20 Aug 1858 W Jeckling sold **64** to Thomas William Powditch master mariner of Wells. 8 Apr 1867 T W Powditch sold **64** to Thomas Powditch junior master mariner of Wells.
Apr 1868 lost at sea.

SEAFLOWER of Wells
13 tons, 33.6 ft, 11.9 ft, 5.6 ft, built 1843 by John Lubbock at Wells, smack, running bowsprit. Master: Thomas Crawford 1843.
SR 6/1843 2 Oct 1843 John Crawford **32** fisherman (and skipper 11 Mar 1844), Robert Crawford **16** fisherman and Jonathon Shreeve **16** carpenter (presumably the same Shreeve who was a shipwright and landlord of the *Jolly Sailor* 1845-61, all of Wells.
29 Mar 1850 registry cancelled as under 15 tons.

SEAGULL of Sheringham
13 tons, 32.3 ft, 10.9 ft, 5.2 ft, built before 1835 at Sheringham?, 3 masted lugger, round stern, clench build.
SR 13/ 1835 & 7/1839 6 June 1839 Henry Ramey Upcher **48** Esquire of Sheringham Hall and Robert Bishop **16** fisherman and skipper of Sheringham.
8 Aug 1861 vessel sold.
The Upchers took a great interest in the welfare of the local fishermen and provided them with a school, a chapel and a lifeboat.

SHIELD of Cromer
14 tons, 33.7 ft, 11.3 ft, 5 ft, built 1841 by Robert Sunman junior at Sheringham, 3 masted lugger, running bowsprit, round stern, clench build. Master: Joseph Davis 1841, James Budderell 1852.
SR 8/1841 & 5/1852 17 May 1841 Ellis Newstead **64** lighthouse keeper, Cromer. 1 May 1852 E Newstead (field labourer) sold **32** each to Benjamin Curtis carpenter and James Budderell fisherman of N Repps (also skipper and based later at Sidestrand.
1870 broken up.

SHEPHERD of Cromer
60 tons, built 1839, schooner. Owner and master 1865 G Kennedy of Cromer, registered at Lowestoft [Clayton, 1865].

SHEPHERDESS of Bacton
Owned by William Partridge (1818-1884) of Bacton probably between 1865 and 1874.

SHERWOOD RANGER of Cley
160 tons, built 1851 brig? Owned by William Taylor of Cley and registered at Sunderland [Clayton, 1865].
White's 1864 *Norfolk Directory* has a Robert Taylor master mariner of Cley. Could William and Robert be the same person?

SIDNEY CLAUDE of Wells
84 tons, 63.1 ft, 16.9 ft, 9.8 ft, built 1847 by John Lubbock at Wells, Official No. 124, schooner. Master: William Ballard 1847.
SR 1/1847 & 1/1878 17 Feb 1847 Joseph Haycock junior **64** merchant of Wells. 27 Jan 1848 mortgaged to Major, Usborne & Co, corn factors of London for £1000. 18 May 1878 sold to Hammond John Parker **64** shipowner and master of Wells. 27 Jan 1879 H J Parker mortgaged **64** to Alice Nunn widow of Field Dalling for £277 10s+5% interest.
6 Nov 1888 broken up
This was named after Haycock's son and traded extensively in the European trades. 11 Jan 1851 sailed for Dublin with grain, 8 Feb 1851 arrived Hull from Konigsberg 550 quarters of wheat, 20 of tares and 250 mats (Hull Customs Bill of Entry), 4 Jan 1852 sailed from Wells to Dublin with grain, 2 Apr 1861 Newcastle to Stettin 114 (long) tons of coal and 30 Aug 1861 Newcastle to Konigsberg same tonnage of coal (gross freights £60.47 and £36.28) [Osler, 1996]. The grain was almost certainly barley for the Guinness brewery, a regular trade for Wells ships.

SIMEON HARDY of Cley
202 tons, 98.8 ft, 23.2 ft, 13.5 ft, built 1837 at Cork, 3 masted barque, male bust figurehead.
SR 7/1865 (transferred from Cork) James Randall **64** and master.
10 Jan 1866 lost at Deal.

SIR WILFRID of Wells or Blakeney
28 tons fishing smack, Official No. 63118. Transferred from Grimsby. King's Lynn registry 2/1890.

SNIPE of Cley
10 tons, 31 ft, 10.1 ft, 5 ft, built 1836 at King's Lynn, cutter, running bowsprit, clench build.
Master: Russell Baines 1841, Murrell Baines 1845.
SR 1/1841 16 Mar 1841 William and Robin Cooke **32** each millers of Glandford and Thornage.

7 Jan 1899 broken up.
Was the **SNIPE** Cooke's yacht?

SOUTHWICK of Wells
50 tons, 56.6 ft, 13.6 ft, 7.7 ft (Lloyd's 1834 gives tonnage as 61 tons. Could this be another vessel?).
Built 1815 at Sunderland, schooner.
Master: Wickham 1834.
SR 7 1838 Henry Cork Garrett **64** mariner and master of Wells. 4 Sept 1840 H C Garrett sold **64** to Joseph Dix farmer and mariner of Dunwich, Suffolk.
14 Oct 1840 re-registered at Southwold.

SOVEREIGN of Sheringham
13 tons, built 1835 at Sheringham, lugger. Master: John Cooper.
SR 9/1840 18 May 1840 Eliner Breeze **42** victualler and John Bayfield **22** fisherman both of Sheringham. 18 Aug 1847 E Breeze mortgaged **42** to William and Charles Temple merchants of Blakeney for £50.
28 Dec 1859 broken up.

SOVEREIGN of Wells or Blakeney
25 ton fishing smack, 4 crew, Official No. 6728, transferred from Gt Yarmouth to King's Lynn 6/1887.

SPRAY of Brancaster, Cromer and Wells
46 tons, 52.6 ft, 16.9 ft, 6.6 ft, built 5 May 1863 at Stanley Ferry, Yorkshire, billy-boy sloop, round stern, carvel and clench build.
SR 6/1863 James High **64** master mariner of Brancaster. 26 Apr 1863 **64** shares mortgaged to Thomas Southerland merchant of Brancaster and discharged 18 Dec 1863. 16 May 1874 J High died intestate leaving all his shares to his widow Alice. 29 July 1874 Alice High sold **16** each to Hammond Thomas Abbs, master mariner, Ephraim Randall master mariner, Stephen Fitt farmer and William Harman fisherman all of Cromer (is this William Harman the same as the Wells shipowner and fisherman?). 7 Mar 1876 H T Abbs sold **16** to John Plumb Ramm innkeeper (*Red Lion* and brewer) of Wells. E Randall sold **16** to Richard Smith master mariner and W Harman sold his **16** to William Staines Andrew merchant's clerk and Stephen Fitt sold his **16** to John Loynes master mariner all of Wells. 3 June 1879 J Loynes sold **6** to W S Staines, **5** to J P Ramm and **5** to Richard Smith.
Nov 1882 wrecked.

SPERO of Cley
77 tons, schooner? Master: W Bowles [Lloyd's 1834].

SQUIRREL of Blakeney
50 tons, 55.3 ft, 13.7 ft, 7 ft, built 1780 at N Shields, schooner. Master: William Beasley (or Bensley?).
SR 10/1836 (Cley) 22 Apr 1839 Tomas William Temple and Charles Temple **32** each merchants of Blakeney. 27 Apr 1855 the Temples sold **64** to William Wilson shipowner of Scarborough. *Norfolk Chronicle* 1850 12 Jan sailed from Blakeney to Newcastle, 9 Feb sailed from Blakeney to Newcastle, 23 Feb arrived from Newcastle, 2 Mar sailed from Blakeney for Newcastle.

STAG of Wells
88 tons, 61.5 ft, 17.3 ft, 9.3 ft, built 1840 by J H Parker or Park, schooner. Master: Henry Parker 1840.
SR 5/1840 & 9/1843 9 Dec 1840 John Chapman **64** merchant [White's 1945 *Norfolk Directory* also maltster] of Wells and 18 Nov 1842 mortgaged to Johnstone & Co, corn factors London and 28 Nov 1843 discharged. 21 Mar 1844 J Chapman mortgaged **64** to R & J Hewetson, corn factors of London. 12 Aug 1846 R & J Hewetson transferred the mortgage to Gurney, Birkdale & Co's bank at Fakenham from whom J Chapman obtained a second mortgage (no sums mentioned).
1863 lost.
In the sample years' 1845 and 1851 the **STAG** been mainly employed carrying malt to London and returning with general goods. Her name may have come from the stag badge of Whitbreads, one of the great London brewers. Captain Park (or Parker) seems to retained command for a much longer period than usual.

STRANGER of Wells
6 tons, 29.6 ft, 9.9 ft, 4.6 ft, built 1820 at King's Lynn, smack.
SR 9/1846 20 Aug 1846 John Rix **64** master mariner of Wells.
3 June 1847 sold on to John Stevens of Shotley, Suffolk.

STAR of Wells or Blakeney
87tons, schooner?, 5 crew, Official No. 67447.
Transferred from Gt Yarmouth. Lynn Registry 1/1891, transferred to Grimsby 1899.

STUDLEY of Cromer
110 tons, brigantine, built at Selby 1829. Owner and master Ephraim Randall (also part owner of the **SPRAY**), registered at Lowestoft [Clayton, 1865].
A fine model of her by Randall in Cromer Museum.

SURPRIZE of Blakeney
12 tons, 32.4 ft, 10.3 ft, 5 ft 3 in, built at Lowestoft 1822.
SR 3/1847 17 Mar 1847 James Carr **64** fisherman (and skipper) of Blakeney.
Presumably taken off Register at some point as under 15 tons.

SURPRIZE of Wells
19 tons, 33 ft 11 in, 11 ft 6 in, 5 ft 5 in, built 1822 at Southtown, Gt Yarmouth, sloop, running bowsprit. Master: Richard Smith of Wells 1835.
SR 3/1835 23 May 1835 Thomas Smith **64** fisherman of Wells.
31 Mar 1838 registry cancelled transferred to Cley.

SUSANNAH of Blakeney
19 tons, 41.1 ft, 11.9 ft, 6.7 ft, built 1822 at Blakeney, sloop, running bowsprit.
SR 2/1845 5 Apr 1845 Francis Plumb **64** fisherman of Blakeney. 5 Mar 1845 'by a clause of redemption of 6 Jan 1845' and **64** transferred to John Ransome gentleman of Holt. 22 Apr 1848 F Plumb mortgaged **64** to William Cooke, miller of Glandford for £45+interest.
17 Feb sold to Southampton owners and re-registered there.

SYLPH of Wells
79 tons, 70.1 ft, 19.2 ft, 9.1 ft, built at Sunderland 1842 schooner, female bust figurehead.
SR 4/1861 (transferred from Gt Yarmouth) Daniel Brook **64** plasterer and painter of Kirkburton, Yorkshire. 10 Mar 1864 D Brook sold **64** to Frederick George London master mariner of Ipswich.
20 Apr 1865 F G London sold **64** to John Amos How master mariner of Woodbridge. Registry transferred to Woodbridge.

TALISMAN of Blakeney
76 tons, 61.8 ft, 17 ft, 9.6 ft, built1842 at Hartlepool, schooner, female bust figurehead.
SR 1/1843 2 Jan 1843 John Starling **32** merchant and Samuel Starling master mariner (& master of vessel) both of Blakeney. 12 Feb 1843 all **64** shares mortgaged to Lord Hastings of Melton Constable Hall (amount of loan not given) and 8 Sept 1847 mortgage discharged.
15 Nov 1847 re-registered at Boston.

TAMERLANE of Cley
150 tons, 78.5 ft, 18.7 ft, 12.4 ft, built 1817 at Southampton, snow. Master: Thomas Howes.
SR 5/1855 31 Jan 1855 Joseph Muskett senior **21** shipowner of Holt [White's 1845 *Norfolk Directory* grocer and draper], Howard Ramm **20** and Clarke Painter **9** both shipowners of Cley, Francis Park **11** shipowner of Cromer, Joseph Muskett **3** as trustee of the children of Mary Burrell.
1876 broken up.

TAY of Wells
54 tons, built 1816 at Newburgh sloop, owner W Smith of Wells.
Regular trader to Wells 1851. 26 May 1860 stranded at Grainthorpe on passage from Hartlepool to Wells with coal, 4 crew [*Commission for Unseaworthy Ships*, 1873].
Presumably registered at Wells before the start of the surviving Register in 1832.

T BROWN
50 tons tug built at Groningen, Netherlands, King's Lynn register2/ 1900, Official No. 93653.
I doubt whether this tug was ever owned on the North Norfolk coast. She is not in the 1914 Mercantile Navy List.

TEAZER of Wells
95 tons, 64.3 ft, 17.2 ft, 10.7 ft, built 1847 by Henry Thomas Tyrrell at Wells, schooner, female figurehead.
SR 6/1847 20 Apr 1847 Joseph Springall Southgate **40** merchant of Wells, James Atkins **8** master mariner (and master) of Burnham Overy and John Southgate **16** postmaster of Wells.
7 July 1855 sold to Goole owner and registry transferred there.

THE GATHERESS of Sheringham
29 tons, 54.1 ft, 16 ft, 6.8 ft, built 1866 at Spittle Bridge, Yorkshire, 2 masted lugger, carvel and clench build.
SR 8/1866 15 Aug 1866 Benjamin and Henry (also skipper) Johnson both fishermen of Sheringham. 30 Apr 1867 H Johnson mortgaged **32** shares to Mary Ann Bayley, widow of GT Yarmouth for £75+5% interest, discharged 2 Dec 1869. 11 July 1870 H & B Johnson mortgaged **64** shares to James Meadows fish salesman of Cleethorpes for £100+5% interest, discharged 13 Jan 1873.
3 Apr 1875 B & H Johnson sold the vessel to Aaron George fisherman of Gorleston and registry transferred to Gorleston.
This was one of the biggest luggers owned in Sheringham and the Johnsons bought her new and without an initial mortgage. The mortgage from James Meadows hints that she may have been working out of Grimsby because Cleethorpes was the salubrious resort down the coast from Grimsby for the holiday maker and the local rich.

THE LADY SONDES of Blakeney
100 tons, 65 ft, 19 ft, 10 ft, built 23 Jan1840, schooner, female bust figurhead. Master: William Bowles 1840.
SR 1/1840 & 8/1856 Robert John and Randle Brereton **32** each both merchants of Blakeney. 7 July 1856 R J Brereton deceased and his executors Robert and Sarah Pearson of Blakeney and John Brereton of London take on his shares. 8 Sept 1856 R J Brereton's executors transfer **32** to Randle Brereton. 7 Jan 1860 R Brereton mortgaged **64** to Harvey & Co, bankers of Norwich for £2000+5% on this and other ships.
23 Sept lost on passage from Pillau to Hartlepool, 4 crew lost [*Commission for Unseaworthy Ships*, 1873].
3 Oct 1860 registry cancelled 'lost on passage from Konigsberg to W Hartlepool'.

According to the *Norfolk Chronicle* 23 Jan 1840 she was built for 'foreign trade'. The Lady Sondes ('The' was part of her title) was probably the wife of Lord Sondes who inherited the earldom in 1836. The Sondes had seats at Elmham, Norfolk, as well as at Lees Court, Kent and Rockingham Castle, N'hants.

THE RELIANCE of Sheringham
13tons, 32 ft, 11.4 ft, 5.3 ft, built 4 Oct 1841 by Lown & Lown of Sheringham, 2 masted lugger round stern, clench build.
SR 13/1841 & 19/1847 John Cooper **32** (skipper) and William Platten **32** both fishermen of Sheringham. 16 Oct 1841 J Cooper and W Platten sold **22** to Leonard Lown boatbuilder of Sheringham. 25 June 1842 J Cooper sold **21** to W Platten and 25 July 1853 L Lown sold **10** back to W Platten. Re-registered 19/1847 with Thomas Platten gamekeeper of East Beckenham, Norfolk as sole shareholder.
There must be some missing transactions. Perhaps one can infer that William Platten died and Thomas (possibly a son) inherited the shares. Thomas continued to own **THE RELIANCE** until 1859 when she was struck off the Register because she was under 15 tons.

THETIS of Cley
16 tons, 34 ft, 12.5 ft, 5.6 ft, built 1837 at London, sloop, running bowsprit. Master: Robert Hudson.
SR 4/1844, 2/1846 & 11/1852 2 Mar 1844 Robert Cooke Moore **64** merchant of Cley. 14 Mar 1846 R C Moore gentleman sold **64** to Frederick Warnes, fisherman of Blakeney. 17 Mar 1846 F Warnes sold **32** to Anthony Drew farmer of Castle Acre. 28 Mar 1846 F Warnes sold **8** each to Henry Nichols shipowner, Isaac Mann both of Blakeney and Bartholomew Jary mariner of Cley. 17 May 1852 all shareholders sold vessel to William Belcham mariner of Brancaster.
26 July 1862 re-registered at King's Lynn with H Curtis of Sheringham as new owner.

THETIS of Cley 110 tons
62.4 ft, 18 ft, 11.7 ft, built 1839 at Wells, schooner, female bust figurehead.
SR 4/1855 31 Jan 1855 John Muskett **26** shipowner of Holt [Craven's 1856 *Norfolk Directory* grocer and draper Market Place], Harold Ramm **4** shipowner (master mariner), Mary Ramm **4** widow, Samuel Bastard senior **20** shipowner and Samuel Bastard junior **6** master mariner (and master) all of Cley and Thomas Gales **4** gentleman of Letheringsett [Craven's 1856 *Norfolk Directory* merchant's clerk]. 2 Dec 1864 S Bastard sold **4** to S Bastard junior. 13 Nov 1867 J Muskett **26** shares transferred to his widow Ann. 16 June 1868 T Gales sold **4** to S Bastard junior. 4 Aug 1873 Ann Muskett sold **26** to Walter Sumpter surgeon of Cley and surgeon to Erpingham Union and the Coastguard.
1976 registry transferred to London.
The Erpingham Union was the combination of the 32 parishes in the Hundred of North Erpingham to run workhouses at Gimingham and Sheringham

TMP of Wells or Blakeney
45 tons, 63.2 ft, 18.3 ft, 7.8 ft, built at Portreath 1874, iron beams, dandy rig, Official No. 69862.
Transferred from Barnstaple and registered 3/1881 at King's Lynn, Martin Page **64** merchant of Blakeney.

THOMAS of Blakeney
79 tons, 74.7 ft, 19.2 ft, 7.6 ft, foreign built, date unknown, schooner.
SR 5/1859 16 Mar 1859 John Pye **64** innkeeper of Blakeney. 14 Mar 1859 J Pye sold **21** to William Nichols, (merchant's) clerk and **21** to John Thompson master mariner both of Blakeney.
3 Feb 1861 lost off Cromer.
The deal with Nichols and Thompson was signed 2 days before the vessel was registered – an unusual way of proceeding.

THOMAS
50 tons, sloop?, registered at King's Lynn 4/1881 and wrecked 1887.

THOMAS CHALMERS of Blakeney
187 tons, 91.1 ft, 22.2 ft, 14 ft, built 1847 at St Marin's, New Brunswick, brig, man figurehead.
SR 1/1859 5 Jan 1855 William Bensley **64** master mariner of Cley, 30 Apr 1866 W Bensley sold **16** to Willliam Lown butcher of Cley.
17 Jan 1872 lost on the Kentish Knock.
Another vessel of the many exported by Canadian shipbuilders to Great Britain in mid 19th century.

THOMAS AND HENRY of Brancaster
12 tons, 29.1 ft, 11.5 ft, 5.9 ft, built 1843 by John Lubbock, smack, running bowsprit.
SR 5/1843 & 3/1862 14 June 1843 Thomas Lane **64** fisherman of Brancaster. 21 Mar 1862 lengthened to 41.2 ft and widened to 12.8 ft (or latter fore likely to have been re-measured) and altered to smack rig same owner. 13 Mar 1871 T Lane sold **64** to John Kent plumber of King's Lynn and 27 Mar 1884 J Kent died and his shares transferred to his widow.
10 Oct 1884 wrecked on Scolt Head, at the entrance to Brancaster harbour.

THOMAS AND MARTHA of Cromer
96 tons, brig built at Wells 1810 [Malster, 1995: 5]. Master: D Ransom [Lloyd's 1831].

TIBERIAS
Fishing smack or lugger transferred from Scarborough 14/1888 and King's Lynn registry No. 1/1900, Official No. 21317.

TRAVELLER of Blakeny
14 tons, 37.8 ft, 10.3 ft, 5.6 ft, built 1820 at Hull, Official No. 21224, smack, running bowsprit.
SR 3/1944 Thomas Miller **64** fisherman (and skipper) of Blakeney.
22 Feb 1860 sold to Montrose owners and re-registered there.

THREE BETSEYS
46 tons, 53 ft, 13.5 ft, 6.4 ft, built 1838 at Swinton (on the Dearne & Dove Canal), sloop, topping bowsprit, round stern, clench build.
SR 9/1853 29 June 1853 John Gunson merchant and Henry Crafer master mariner (and master) **32** each both of Wells.
Oct 1869 left Wells late one afternoon laden with barley for the Humber, the wind was SW and raining. About 7.00 pm the wind veered to NNW and blew a gale. The shattered billy boy was found next morning scattered along Holkham Beach. All the crew were lost - Captain Ben Marsh, his brother Bircham and James Samphер [Harman, 1995: 24].

TRAFALGAR of Cley
21 tons, 45.3 ft, 13 ft, 5.6 ft, built 1806 at Gt Yarmouth, schooner, carvel and clench build.
SR 1/1858 (transferred from King's Lynn) 22 Jan 1858 Thomas Brown **64** master mariner (and probably master) of Cley. 18 Oct 1871 T Brown sold **64** to William Holroyd merchant of Lowestoft and Holroyd sold it on 4 Nov to John Wake shipowner of Whitby.
11 July 1873 broken up.
It is difficult to know if this was used for fishing or cargo carrying. It is small for the latter and yet it was schooner rigged which would have been unusual in a fishing vessel. It also interesting to see that Gt Yarmouth builders used the carvel and clinker combination which is usually associated with Humber shipbuilders.

TRIAL of Wells
64 tons, 57 ft 6 in, 15 ft 11 in, 7 ft, built 1824 Wells, sloop, hoisting up bowsprit, round stern. Master: Robert Munson 1832-1845.
SR 15/1832, 9/1833, 15/1836 & 6/1845 4 Sept 1853 Joseph Springall Southgate **64** shipowner (and merchant) of Wells, 22 Sept 1832 **64** shares mortgaged to Gurney, Birkbeck & Co bankers, Fakenham. 27 July 1833 bankers transferred mortgage to George Crofts merchant of Wells. 5 Sept 1833 G Crofts sold **64** to J H Parker, shipbuilder of Wells. 12 Sept 1833 J H Parker mortgaged **64** to John Savory miller of Burnham Overy and 17 June 1835 took out a second mortgage with J Savory for £150 due to him. Dec 1841 G Crofts still had mortgage with J Savory. 21 July 1845 sold **32** each to Robert Munson master mariner (and master) and Henry John Cross merchant both of Wells and H J Cross continued mortgage of £490+5% interest from previous registration.
1846 lost at sea.
The **TRIAL** ran a regular London packet service eg made 8 round voyages in 1845. She was replaced by the **DESPATCH**.

TRIAL of Bacton or Cromer (probably)
11 tons, 32 ft, 10 ft, 4.9 ft, built at 1840 Ludham, 2 masted lugger , running bowsprit, round stern, clench build.
Master: John Haylett 1840, James Hook 1845, Joseph Davis 1847.
SR 21/1840,6/1845 & 14/1847 30 Dec 1840 Robert Cubitt **64** farmer of Ridlington (4m East of N Walsham & not on the coast), 25 July 1845 R Cubitt sold **64** to Robert Bullen innkeeper of Cromer and 17 July 1847 R Bullen sold **32** each to Joseph & William Davison fishermen of Cromer who continue to own her until broken up in 1870.

TWEEDSIDE of Cley
254 tons, 112.2 ft, 27.8 ft, 13.2 ft, built 1854 at Wallace, Nove Scotia, brig.
7/1863 (transferred from London) 29 June 1863 James William Porritt **64** shipowner (& merchant) of Cley and same day J N Porritt sold **8** to Thomas Dew master mariner of Blakeney and probably her master) and **16** Christmas Jarvis Sturgess (spelled Starges in register as pronounced locally). Nov 1865 T Dew mortgaged **8** shares to J N Porritt for £100+5% interest.
19 Mar 1875 lost off Gt Yarmouth.
Another vessel exported by Canadian shipbuilders to Great Britain in the mid 19th century. Hooton has a fine painting of her and a photograph on a patent slip at Ipswich [Hooton, 1996:245-6].

TWO BROTHERS of Wells
86 tons, 67.4 ft, 19.9 ft, 6.1 ft, built 1796 Limehouse, barge or sloop. Master: Robert Cook 1832.
SR 10/1832 (transferred from Harwich) 2 June 1832 John Lubbock **64** shipbuilder of Wells.
13 June 1835 broken up.
Barge suggests that she was flat-bottomed with a sloop rig. It is unclear why Lubbock acquired this vessel unless was to repair her and sell her on.

TWO BROTHERS of Blakeney
13 tons, 32 ft, 10.11 ft, 5.1 ft, built 1800, River Itchen, sloop, running bowsprit.
SR 12/1843 14 Sept 1843 Thomas Johnson **64** fisherman (and skipper) of Blakeney.
23 Oct 1855 registry cancelled as under 15 tons.

TWO BROTHERS of Wells & Blakeney
35 tons 53.6 ft, 14.3 ft, 6.1 ft, built 1828 at Wakefield (on River Calder), billy-boy sloop, top up bowsprit, round stern.
SR 9/1852 & 4/1864 16 June 1852 Robert Thomas **42** master mariner (master of vessel) and Robert Garlick **22** shipbroker of Knottingley and R Garlick sold **32** to R Thomas. 14 Dec 1864 sold to Robert Cubitt **32** and John Starling **32** both merchants of Blakeney.
10 Dec 1871 registry cancelled converted into lighter.

TWO BROTHERS of Wells
36 tons, 52.3 ft, 12.5 ft, 5.2 ft, built 1825 by Joseph Slight at Brigg, Lincs, sloop, round stern, clench build. Master: Robert Temple 1841, Race Hammond 8 Dec 1842, William Temple 1846.
SR 1/1841 & 1846 5 Mar 1841 Robert Temple senior master mariner and 13 Sept 1841 mortgaged to William Harman, merchant of Wells. 10 Mar 1846 R Temple died and left **64** shares to William Temple master mariner (subject to mortgage), 18Mar 1850 mortgage discharged. 19 Mar 1850 **64** mortgaged to William Nettleton Gardner on security for £50+interest, and discharged 9 June 1854. 1863 owned by John Smith of Bacton, registered at Lowestoft, on a regular coal run, averaging 15 voyages Mar to Oct Hartlepool to Bacton [Malster, 1995: 5].
1865 converted to river lighter.
William Harman 1781-1866 was a mariner, turned shipowner, innkeeper and property owner in Wells and W G Gardner was a local farmer.

TWO BROTHERS of Blakeney
42 tons, 56 ft, 13.1 ft, 6 ft, built 1840 by Arthur Richards at King's Lynn, sloop, topping up bowsprit, round stern, carvel and clench build. Master: Edward Ulton 1840.
SR 12/1840 8 June 1840 William Cooke **32** miller of Glandford and Robin Cooke **32** miller of Thornage, 23 Apr 1841 W Cooke & R Cooke sold **5** each to Edward Ulton master mariner of Blakeney.
8 Feb 1855 re-registered at Gt Yarmouth.

TWO BROTHERS of Wells
24 tons, 44.9 ft, 13.12 ft, 6.3 ft built 1841 at Scarborough, yawl (later a sloop), round stern, clench build.
SR 5/1866 13 Mar 1866 Edmond Mabell **16** coal merchant Binham, James Savory **32** and Henry Savory **16** mariners of Wells. Feb 1867 Henry Savory sold **16** to J Savory. 25 Feb 1867 Edmond Mabell sold **16** to J Savory. 31 Dec 1868 J Savory sold **64** to John Savory miller, maltser and merchant of Burnham Overy.
Feb 1875 lost in collision in Humber.
An ex-fishing vessel.

TWO BROTHERS of Wells
91 tons, 62 ft, 17.1 ft, 9.4 ft, built 1842 at Wells by J H Parker, schooner, round stern. Master: Thomas Walker 1842, Robert W Hammond 2 Jan 1845 at London, John Durrant 10 Dec 1850 at Cley, John Innes 13 Apr 1854 (Newcastle).
SR 6/1842 25 July 1842 Thomas Powditich **42** master mariner of Wells and John Powditch **22** shipwright. 1877 broken up.

TWO BROTHERS of Cromer
10 tons, 33 ft, 11.2 ft, 4.8 ft, built 1842 at Cromer by John Rogers, 2 masted lugger, running bowsprit, round stern, clench build. Master: William Mayes 1842.
SR 7/1842 1 Aug 1842 William Mayes and Gilbert Mayes **32** each fishermen of Cromer.
1865 sold to Boston owners, 29 Dec 1880 registry cancelled.

TWO BROTHERS of Wells or Blakeney
17 tons, fishing vessel, 3 crew, transferred from Shorham to King's Lynn 2/1887.

TWO BROTHERS AND FRIENDS of Burnham Overy
10 tons, 29.6 ft, 10.3 ft, 5.3 ft, built 1829 at Burnham Overy, smack, running bowsprit, clench build. Master: Joseph Parr.
SR 6/1844 15 Apr 1844 William Parr **48** and Joseph Parr **16** fishermen of Burnham Overy.
December 1859 registry cancelled as under 15 tons.

TWO FRIENDS of Cley
44 tons, 55.65 ft, 16.58 ft, 6.78 ft, built at Wells 1838, sloop, round stern.
SR 4/1866 23 Mar 1866 John Turner and John Ellis Turner **48** merchants of Cley. David Parlett **16** master mariner of Salthouse. 10 Mar 1875 the Turners sold **48** to J Ellis Turner & Sidney Turner merchants of Cley
27 July 1875 all shareholders sold **64** to Isaac Jackson shipowner of Goole, registry transferred to Goole.
Norwich Mercury 1841 entered Lowestoft for ballast after delivering coal to Sheringham.

TWO SISTERS of Wells
42 tons, 54.7 ft, 12.8 ft, 5.8 ft, built 1822 at Brigg, billy-boy sloop, topping bowsprit, round stern.
Master: John Harman 1838, John Cocker, Goole 24 Apr 1841, Thomas Thrush, Lynn 15 Feb 1848, Nicholas, Austwick 4 Mar 1849, John Walker 20 Oct 1849 Lynn, George Fleck 7 Mar 1850 Lynn.
SR 8/1838 & 11/1838 Thomas and Sarah Stone **48** bakers of Stiffkey and John Harman **16** mariner of Wells.
The changes of master suggest her main routes.

TWO SISTERS of Wells
40 tons, 54.7 ft, 12.5 ft, 5.9 ft, built 1827 at Barton-on-Humber, billy-boy sloop, round stern, clench build. Master: Robert Temple junior 1841.
SR 5/1841 & 6/1846 13 Apr 1841 Robert Temple senior **64** shipowner, 13 Sept 1841 mortgaged to William Harman of Wells. R Temple apparently from Barton-on-Humber according to his will 16 Jan 1845, and 10 Mar 1846 **64** shares left to Robert Temple junior subject to mortgage which was discharged 19 Apr 1850 and same day mortgaged to William Nettleton Gardner 'in security only'.
25 Mar 1854 lost at sea.

ULYSSES of Wells
59 tons, 55.1 ft, 16.3 ft, 8.1 ft, built 1842 at Prince Edward Island, Canada, schooner, billet head.
SR 11/1846 8 Oct 1846 William Cooke **64** master mariner (and master of this vessel) of Wells and same day mortgaged to John Lubbock shipbuilder of Wells, and discharged 22 Mar 1848 (amount of loan not specified).
19 Jan 1860 lost off Hartlepool.
6 Apr 1850 sailed from Wells in ballast for Hartlepool for coal, 6 July 1850 and 7 Sept 1850 'sailed northwards' in ballast, 30 Nov sailed for Hartlepool in ballast, arrived back 21 Dec from Hartlepool with coal. The **ULYSSES** should be designated a collier on the basis of this sample because she only collected coal cargoes. Canadian shipbuilders exported many vessels to British shipowners in the mid 19th century. PEI specialised in building the smaller vessels.

UNDINE of Wells
6 tons, 36.2 ft, 8.8 ft, 3.9 ft, built at Ipswich 7 Oct 1850, sloop.
SR 4/1867 27 June 1867 Hugh Robert Rump **64** gentleman of Wells [White's 1864 Directory surgeon].
23 Sept 1890 existence of vessel doubtful.
The **UNDINE** was a yacht and given her small size probably used for day sailing from Wells.

UNION of Blakeney
34 tons, 49.4 ft, 16.9 ft, 6.5 ft, built 1833, Sutton, Yorkshire, billy-boy ketch, round stern, carvel and clench build.
Master: Francis Cushing 1867.
SR 6/1866 & 6/1867 31 Mar 1866 Robert Cubitt Wells **64** merchant of Blakeney. Re-registered 1 Dec 1867 after lengthening 46 tons, 61.4 ft, 16.9 ft, 6.6 ft. 9 Dec 1874 R C Wells died and his shares inherited by his widow Harriet and Augustus Hill farmer of Blakeney who became managing owner.
1 Mar 1878 lost of the Mouse light vessel.

VENTURE of Wells 104 tons
74.2 ft, 18.1 ft, 9.6 ft, built 1848 by Robuste at Bayonne & lengthened at Wells 1853, schooner (30 Aug 1856 converted to brigantine), scroll figurehead. Master: Edward Bunting 1853, William Belcham 24 Oct 1854.
SR 4/1853 26 Apr 1853 William Nettleton Gardner **11** gentleman [White's 1845 *Norfolk Directory* farmer], Henry Thomas Tyrrell **11** shipowner (shipbuilder), Robert Cubitt **11** merchant, John Powditch **11** shipowner (shipwright), Thomas Powditch **10** shipowner (master mariner), John Smith **10** shipowner (master mariner) all of Wells.
1875 sold to King's Lynn owners and re-registered there.

VERACITY of Wells
55 tons, 61.4 ft, 16.8 ft, 8.1 ft, built 1830 at Bideford, schooner.
SR 2/1864 transferred from Colchester 1 July 1864 William Smith **64** merchant of Wells. 11 Aug 1864 W Smith sold **21** shares to James Elenor ship carpenter of Wells. 20 Apr 1867 W Smith mortgaged **43** shares to James William Smith master mariner and discharged 8 Mar 1873. 5 Mar 1873 J Elener sold **21** to J Smith.
24 Nov 1882 W Smith sold **64** J W Smith and re-registered at King's Lynn 14/1882.

VICTOR of Wells or Blakeney
20 tons, fishing smack, Official No. 52892, King's Lynn registry 1/1894.

VICTORIA of Runton
25 tons, 41 ft, 13.8 ft, 6.4 ft, built 1840 at Scarborough, lugger, running bowsprit, round stern, clench build.
SR 7/1840 12 May 1840 William Grimes **32** fisherman, John Grimes **16** fisherman (& skipper) and John Dennis **16** farmer all of Runton. 11 July 1842 J Dennis sold **4** to J Grimes.
15 Mar 1854 re-registered at Gt Yarmouth (new owners?).

VICTORY of Runton
8 tons, 30.7 ft, 9.9 ft, 4 ft, built 1829 at Sheringham, 3 masted lugger, running bowsprit, square stern, clench build.
SR 2/1840 20 Feb 1840 Matthew Abbs **32** fisherman (and skipper), James Lome **16** fisherman, Maria Riseborough **16** spinster all of Runton.
24 Feb 1864 broken up 1861 and registry cancelled.

VICTORY of Sheringham
12 ton lugger, registered at Cley 20/1837, broken up 1868.

VIVID of Wells
91 tons, 72.4 ft, 17.4 ft, 10.7 ft, built 1842 at Stockton on Tees, schooner, man's bust figurehead & removed at Faversham 8 Mar 1859.
Master: Robert Elliot 1847.
SR 13/1847 12 July 1847 Edward Elliot **64** shipowner [White's 1845 Norfolk Directory master mariner].
19 Mar 1866 transferred to Lowestoft register.

WARRIOR of Blakeney
75.1 ft, 16.8 ft, 8.6 ft, 49 hp, built 1866 at S Shields paddle tug, sloop round stern clench built.
SR1/1872 18 Apr 1872 John Ellis Turner **64** merchant of Blakeney. 17 April 1872 J E Turner sold shares to the following: Robert Cubitt Wells merchant **7**, Samuel Daniels **2** shipowner, William Starling **5** merchant, Robert Henry Allen **1** blacksmith,, Henry Mallett **1** grocer, Benjamin Henry Nichols **2** merchant, William Isaac Bensley **2** shipowner (& master mariner), George Thompson **1**

master mariner, Charles Temple **5** master mariner, James Power **1** master mariner and James William Porritt **5** shipowner – ALL of Blakeney. 17 May 1872 Robin (or Robert?) Cooke **4** merchant (shipowner, miller & farmer) of Glandford, Randle Barwick Brereton **4** clerk in holy orders Stiffkey, Martin Fountain Page **7** merchant of Brinton and William Henry Tillett **4** solicitor of Sprowston. 24 May 1872 Thomas Burton **4** shipbroker of Seaham. 9 Dec 1874 R C Wells dies and left **7** shares to his widow and executor Augustus Hill farmer of Blakeney.
28 June 1876 all shareholders agreed to sell the vessel to John Batey steam tug owner of Newcastle and re-registered there.
Page and Turner became a partnership of merchants and shipowners and presumably had links through families, friendships or business links to this miscellaneous bunch of shareholders. Some already owned shares in ships e.g Robin Cooke or William Starling. No doubt the Rev Brereton was related to the merchants of that surname at Blakeney. As Rector of Stiffkey and Morston, he enjoyed the considerable stipend of £800 pa [White's 1845 *Norfolk Directory*].

WASHINGTON of Wells
115 tons, 67 ft 2 in, 19 ft 10 in, 10 ft 4 in, built 1828 at Wells, brig. Master: Miles Jarvis 1833.
SR 10/1833 & 4/1837 1 7 Sep 1833 John Bulling **52** farmer of Holkham, Robert Powell **8** mariner of Brancaster and Thomas Bloom **8** mariner of Goole. Re-registered 30 June 1837 no change in shareholders. 16 Sept 1837 T Bloom sold **4** shares to Mile Jarvis master. 10 June 1841 re-registered at Hull probably with change of owneship.

WATERLOO (ex **PRINCIPE CELESTE**) of Cley
147 tons, 70.7 ft, 23.6 ft, 14.4 ft, built date unknown at Pinico de Torento, Naples, brig, male bust removed or lost 13 Feb 1860.
SR 4/1857 24 Apr 1857 James William Porritt **64** merchant of Cley. 3 Mar 1879 J W Porritt sold all **64** shares to William Stoker ship's agent South Shields, re-sold and re-registered at S Shields.

WAVE of Blakeney
11 tons, 76.2 ft, 20.4 ft, 10.9 ft, built 22 Apr 1856 at Arbroath, schooner, female bust figurehead.
SR 8/1865 (transferred from Arbroath) 8 Dec 1865 Samuel Daniel **64** master mariner of Blakeney, 27 Dec 1865 S Daniel sold **8** to Charles Temple shipowner of Blakeney.
19 Mar 1866 collided with the **DARING** of Jersey and sank.

WAVE of Wells or Blakeney
198 tons, schooner, Official No. 2650, King's Lynn registry 3/1890.

WELCOME HOME of Brancaster
40 tons, 57.3 ft 14.5 ft, 6.8 ft, built 1847 at Worsborough Dale, Yorks, billy-boy sloop, round stern, carvel and clench build.
SR 1/1862 (transferred from Goole) 5 Feb 1862 Henry Mussett **32** master mariner and Elizabeth Mussett **32** widow both of Brancaster.
31 Jan 1874 registry cancelled sold for use as a river lighter at Leeds.

WELCOME HOME of Brancaster
47 tons, 60.2 ft, 17 ft, 7.1 ft, built 1872 at Stanley Ferry, Yorkshire, ketch? round stern, probably a billy-boy.
SR 2/1872 30 Sept 1872 Henry Mussett **43** master mariner (managing owner & master) and Joseph Dowdy **21** master mariner both of Brancaster. 4 June 1874 J Dowdy sold **21** shares to H Mussett.
2 June 1881 H Mussett sold **64** to Henry Burkill coal merchant of Ferriby Sluice, Lincs and re-registered at Hull.

WELCOME MESSENGER of Runton
10 tons, 33.3 ft, 10.3 ft, 4.9 ft, built at Sheringham 1829, Official No. 67800, 3 masted lugger, running bowsprit, round stern, clench build.
SR 9/1851 28 July 1851 John Love **64** fisherman (and skipper) of Runton.
1869 registry closed, broken up.

WELLESLEY of Wells or Blakeney
67 tons, schooner?, Official No. 65848, King's Lynn registry 1/1898.

WELLS PACKET of Wells
68 tons, 57 ft, 16 ft 5 in, 8 ft 4 in, built 1833 by John Lubbock at Wells, sloop, round stern.
Master: Richard Lord (& owner) 1833, Robert Cook 5 Apr 1837, John Watson 30 Aug 1838, Robert Mussett 4 Oct 1847, James Smith 22 Aug 1848 at Hartlepool, Randall 1865.
SR 11/1833, 7/1849 & 2/1855 26 Oct 1833 Richard Lord **64** mariner of Wells, 22 Apr 1836 Richard Lord transferred **64** shares to Charlotte Lord spinster. 15 Jan 1855 C Lord transferred **64** to R Lord (bill of sale 5 Dec 1854). 9 Jan 1855 re-rigged as schooner and 25 Sept 1862 R Lord mortgaged **64** shares to Robert Michael Hammond gentleman of Fakenham and Henry Tyrrell of Wells for £50+6% interest.
17 Mar transferred to Lowestoft as R Lord had moved to Southwold [Clayton, 1865].
Arrived at Wells from Newcastle with coal, 18 Jan 1845, 22 Feb, 15 Mar, 12 Apr, 26 Apr, 24 May, 7 June, 21 June, 5 July, 30 Aug, 20 Sept, 4 Oct, 22 Nov, 20 Dec, and all her outward sailings were in ballast. In other words she was a regular 'collier' and not a 'packet' collecting or delivering small parcels of goods and passengers.

WENSLEYDALE of Cromer
56 tons, 59.4 ft, 14.5 ft, 8.1 ft, built 1813 at Goole, schooner. Master: Thomas Holmes 1849.
SR 5/1849 13 Apr 1849 Jeremiah Cross **64** shipowner of Overstrand [White's 1845 *Norfolk Directory* coal merchant at Cromer i.e. private residence at Overstrand].
1878 sold and transferred to Hartlepool.

Some North Norfolk vessels traded afar. The Mediterranean and the Baltic from London or Newcastle were their main destinations. The **NORFOLK TAR** *was built in 1848 at Tyrrell's yard, Wells and traded to ports such as Alicante and Riga.. Here she was being towed through the Avon Gorge to Bristol Docks (Bristol Museums)*

The **WENSLEYDALE** was a regular collier at Cromer but as the Great Eastern Railway arrived at the town in 1877, coal merchants switched their deliveries on to the rails [Malster, 1995:6]. Malster also had her building place as Paull on the Humber.

WHEATHILL of Wells
76 tons, 62 ft 1 in, 16 ft 7 in, 8 ft 5 in, built 1831 at Wells, sloop, round stern. Master: H Park 1832.
SR 21/1832 3 Dec 1832 James Chapman **64** merchant of Wells, and same day mortgaged to James Sharp Giles & Edward Sidgwick corn factors of London. 28 Dec 1840 mortgage renewed with J S Giles and the executors of E Sidgwick. 28 Dec 1840 J Chapman sold **64** to John Dodman merchant of King's Lynn. 1839 Pigot's *Norfolk Directory* named this ship and the **WHIM** as London traders alternately every fortnight. 8 Apr 1841 registry cancelled at Wells.
26 Dec 1852 abandoned on passage Grangemouth to Hartlepool, 4 crew, James Reeve owner [*Commission on Unseaworthy Ships* 1873].

WHIM of Wells
77 tons, 62 ft 3 in, 16 ft 8 in, 8 ft 4 in, built 1832 at Wells, schooner, round stern.
Master: Robert Hall 1832,James Sturley 1835, Thomas Powditch 18 July 1835 –1845, H Gay 1865.
Sr 20/1832, 2/1835, 7/1835, 13/1836 & 5/1845 21 Nov 1832 Joseph Springall Southgate **64** shipowner (and merchant) of Wells. 17 Feb 1833 J S Southgate sold **16** to Henry Proudfoot gentleman of Stanhoe [White's 1845 *Norfolk Directory* farm bailiff], 6 Feb 1834 H Proudfoot sold **16** back to J S Southgate, and the following day J S Southgate 'conditionally' mortgaged **16** shares to H Proudfoot. 18 Sept 1834 J S Southgate mortgaged **64** to Thomas Pooley, merchant of Norwich. 27 Aug 1835 with mortgages presumably discharged J S Southgate sold **64** to George Crofts shipowner (& merchant) of Wells. 28 Aug 1835 G Crofts mortgaged **64** shares to H Proudfoot for £370+ interest and also to John Savory miller of Burnham Overy for £100+interest. This mortgages were renewed up till 28 Aug 1836 and after 11 Dec 1839 the loan seems to have been from J Savory alone. 21 July 1845 J Savory (who must have foreclosed the mortgage) sold **42** shares to Henry John Crofts and **22** to Thomas Powditch master mariner (& master). H J Crofts mortgaged his **42** shares to J Savory for £490+5% interest. 31 Oct 1853 H J Crofts discharged mortgage to J Savory and re-mortgaged **43** shares to J S Southgate 'to secure balance of account owed to J S Southgate by H J Crofts. By 1865, the vessel was owned by T Powditch according to Clayton although this is not mentioned in the main register.
1879 broken up.
Pigot's 1839 *Norfolk Directory* lists the **WHIM** and the **WHEATHILL** as regular fortnightly traders to London. By 1845, she was no confined to sailings only to London. *Norfolk Chronicle* 1845 arrivals 11 Jan from Goole coal, 15 Feb London, 15 Mar Goole, 19 Apr London, 5 July Goole goods, 16 Aug London, 20 Sept London goods. Her outward sailings seem to have been in ballast to London, Newcastle, Seaham etc. Only 8 Dec report mentioned she was carrying barley and goods for London.

WILLIAM AND ANNE of Blakeney
88 tons, 60 ft, 16.7 ft, 10.7 ft, built 1819 at Monkwearmouth, schooner, female bust figurehead. Master: William Mayes 1843.
SR 9/1843 William Keymer **24** farmer of Salthouse, Robert Pegg **24** Farmer of Themelthorpe and Ann Frankling **16** spinster of Themelthorpe.
10 Mar 1844 re-registered at Yarmouth (with same owners?).

WILLIAM AND ANN of Wells
20 tons, 43.8 ft, 13.9 ft, 7.6 ft, built 8 May 1840 at Wells, smack.
SR 1/1860 8 May 1860 William Green **64** fisherman of Wells. 22 Sept 1862 W Green mortgaged **64** shares to Samuel Waters solicitor of Little Walsingham and discharged 24 Apr 1867. 30 June 1874 W Green mortgaged **64** shares to Harriet Leeds of E Dereham for £180+5% interest and discharged 8 Sept 1879. Same day sold to Wells Fishing Co, the Post Office Staithe St, Wells and 17 Mar 1883 re-sold to Francis Kerrison master mariner of Blakeney.
2 Oct 1891 registry cancelled.

WILLIAM AND CHARLES of Brancaster
8 tons, 26.4 ft, 6.4 ft, 4.9 ft, built 1833 at King's Lynn, cutter, running bowsprit.
SR 2/1845 15 Feb 1845 Charles Anness **64** mariner (& master) of Brancaster.
22 Aug 1866 re-registered at King's Lynn.

WILLIAM AND GEORGE of Wells
25 tons, 45.5 ft, 12 ft, 6.6 ft, built 1833 at Wells , smack, running bowsprit.
Master: Robert Frankling 1836, Thomas Field 14 Feb 1842, John Hayden 31 Jan 1843.
SR 23/1836 & 10/1841 23 Aug 1836 John Lubbock **43** shipbuilder of Wells, William Bourne **21** merchant of Erpingham. 20 Nov 1845 W Bourne deceased and his executors (J Lubbock & Harriet Bourne) sold **64** shares to William Waters farmer of Wighton. 10 Jan 1844 W Waters sold **64** to W Hocking, mariner of Burnham (on-Crouch).
2 Mar 1844 re-registered at Maldon.

WILLIAM AND JOHN of Blakeney?
Brig, owned by William Allen of Weybourne 1873-75.
Went ashore 5th Oct 1875 on passage from Cronstadt to Dover and probably abandoned [Mills,1957: 133 & 134 water colour and log].

WILLIAM AND MARY of Cromer
11 tons, 33 ft? 10.2 ft, 5 ft, built 1835 at Sheringham, lugger, running bowsprit, round stern, clench build. Master: William Rix 1840.
SR 10/1840 20 May 1840 William Sunman? **64** fisherman of Cromer.
17 Mar 1886 registry cancelled, broken up.

WILLIAM BLAGDEN of Brancaster
38 tons, 56.4 ft, 14.7 ft, 6.7 ft, built 9 June 1843 at Sheffield, billy-boy sloop, round stern, clench build.
SR 5/1857 25 May 1857 Samuel Powditch **64** master mariner of Brancaster.
17 Nov 1880 cut down to river craft.

WILLIAM THE FOURTH of Wells
26 tons, 46.6 ft 13.7 ft, 6.6 ft, built 1830 at Lowestoft, 3 masted lugger, running bowsprit, clench build.
SR 18/1850 12 Dec 1850 Edmund Sturley **64** master mariner (& master) of Wells. 20 Sept 1853 E Sturley mortgaged **64** shares for £31 5s 6d +interest from C D & John B Charlesworth, coal merchants of Lofthouse, Yorks.

WILLIAM THE FOURTH of Cley
63 tons, 57 ft, 15 ft, 8 ft, built 1830 at Wells schooner, round stern. Master: Zacharias Baines1845-50+.
SR 21/1836 (Cley), 7/1845 & 7/1850 27 Nov 1845 Margaret Moore **40** widow [White's 1845 *Norfolk Directory* merchant] and Thomas Beckwith **24** clerk in Holy Orders (and curate of Wiveton) of Cley. 6 Apr 1850 all **64** shares sold to Z Baines (master) of Wells and same day Z Baines took out a mortgage on them with Margaret Moore for £189 10s+5% interest. This was discharged 18 Nov 1854. Transferred to S Shields 17 Jan 1859.
1 Nov 1861 wrecked in collision in Yarmouth Roads on passage from Shields to Lowestoft, crew of 4 saved, owner Z Baines [*Commission for Unseaworthy Ships*, 1873].

WYE of Blakeney
148 tons, 81 ft, 20 ft, 11 ft, built 1848 at Brockswear, Glos. Brig, male bust figurehead. Master: W Beart 1865.
SR 10/1855 (transferred from London) 16 June 1855 William Patrick **16** butcher and William Smith **16** grocer both of Newcastle, William and Charles Temple **12** each merchants of Blakeney and Daniel (or David) Thomas **8** shipowner (master mariner) of Blakeney. 1867 Charles Temple sold 16 to T J Starling of Blakeney.

YARE of Cromer
82 tons, 5 shares offered for sale in *Norwich Mercury* 10 Feb 1810 [Malster, 1995:5].

YOUNG MAN'S INDUSTRY of Wells
Built King's Lynn 1824, probably smack.
SR 1/1839 28 Mar 1839 John Coe **64** master mariner of Wells. 4 Apr 1872 J Coe sold **64** to Miles Edward Palmer and Frederick William Whitaker shipwrights of Wells. 20 Apr 1877 M E Palmer sold **32** to F W Whitaker.
12 Dec 1894 registry cancelled, vessel unseaworthy.

ZEBRINA of Wells
92 tons, built at Sunderland 1828.
Master and part owner Isaac Mann.
'Latest voyage Cley to Newcastle' [Lloyd's 1834].

ZOAR of Cromer
9 tons, 32.5 ft, 10.4 ft, 5 ft, built 1836 at Sheringham, 3 masted lugger, running bowsprit, round stern, clench build.
Previous transaction Henry Hales **64** fisherman (& skipper) sold **32** to Ellis Newstead Field lighthouse keeper of Cromer. This must have been a mortgage because by Mar 1847 Hales had all **64** shares again.
SR 5/1847 22 Mar 1847 Henry Hales **48** fisherman (& skipper) and John Long **16** fisherman both of Cromer.
Lost at sea 28 Oct 1861, 9 crew drowned, W West owner [*Commission for Unseaworthy Ships*, 1873].

ZOAR of Sheringham
30 tons, 48.9 ft, 14.11 ft, 6.5 ft, built 1847 by James Beeching at Gt Yarmouth.
SR 10/1847 John (also skipper) and Robert Cock **32** each fisermen of Sheringham. 18 Dec 1854 R Cock sold his **32** shares to J Cock for £60 (bill of sale 12 Aug 1850).
15 Mar 1854 re-registered at Gt Yarmouth.

Bibliography

Catling M, 'The Bluejacket' in ***Norfolk Sailor***, vol. 10 (1965).

Clapson R, ***A Lincolnshire Shipyard – Burton upon Stather***, Barton on Humber, 2007.

Clayton W, Register of Shipping, Hull, 1865.

Daniel J, ***Directory of Port Charges***, London, 1856.

Dobson S, 'Stormy Weather: the Ramms of Cley in the early 19th century' in ***The Glaven Historian***, No 12 (2010) 32-45.

Fiddian V (ed), ***Salthouse, the Story of a Norfolk Village***, Salthouse, 2003.

Finch R, ***Coals from Newcastle***, Lavenham 1973.

Gosney R & Bowyer R, ***The Sailing Ships and Mariners of Knottingley***, Knottingley c.2000.

Harman W, 1854-1944 ***Memoirs***, Wells, 1995.

Hooton J, ***The Glaven Ports***, Blakeney 1996.

Hooton J, 'The ANN of Clay, Capt. Francis Plumb' in ***The Glaven Historian***, No. 6 (2003) 15-19.

Hooton J, 'The Catling ship models' in ***The Glaven Historian***, No.10 (2007) 23-28.

Jefferson R, 'W J J Bolding (1815-1899) Pioneer North Norfolk Photographer' in ***The Glaven Historian***, No 6 (2003) 3-14.

Lloyd's List

Malster R, ***Wherries and Waterways***, Lavenham 1871.

Malster R, ***Saved from the Sea***, Lavenham 1974.

Malster R, 'The 19th Century Maritime Trade of Cromer and other minor East Anglian ports', in Longcroft A & Joby R, ***East Anglian Studies***, Norwich 1995.

March E, ***Sailing Trawlers***, London 1953.

Mellor D, ***The Glaven Valley – More Historical Jottings***, Glandford 1992.

Mills J F C, 'Merchant Shipping' in ***Norfolk Maritime History Exhibition'***, Castle Museum, Norwich 1957, 11-16.

Norfolk Chronicle

Norfolk News

Osler A, personal communication, 20 Nov 1998.

Paget-Tomlinson E W, ***The Complete Book of Canal and River Navigations***, Albrighton, 1978.

Purchas A W, ***Some History of Wells-Next-The -Sea and District***, Ipswich, 1965.

Prentice R, ***Celebration of the Sea***, London, 1994.

Stammers M K, 'The Hand Maiden and Victim of Agriculture: the port of Wells-Next-The-Sea, Norfolk in the Eighteenth and Nineteenth Centuries' in ***Mariner's Mirror***, 86 (2000), 60-68.

Stammers MK, 'Blakeney Ships and their Owners in the mid 19th century' in ***Glaven Historian***, 10 (2007), 17-22.

Stammers M K, 'The Rope Archive' in ***Mariner's Mirror***, 94 (2008), 94-97.

Stammers M K, ' A maritime snapshot of a rural port in the Mid Nineteenth Century, Wells-Next-The-Sea, Norfolk in ***Mariner's Mirror***, 95 (2009), 317-326.

Stammers M K, ***Shipbuilding at Wells in the 18th and 19th centuries***, Wells, 2011.

Welland M, ***The History of the Inns & Public Houses of Wells***, Wells, 2012.